Sarah's Quest:

A Place to Belong

Book II of Hannah's Legacy

By Cary Flanagan

Publisher:

Cary Flanagan

ISBN# 978-1-7374754-3-9

This book is a work of fiction. Names, characters, places, and incidents are products of the author's imagination or are used fictitiously. Any resemblance to actual events, places, or persons, living or dead, is entirely coincidental.

Also, By Cary Flanagan:

"Moon Dance – A Quilter's Creative Journey"

Twelve Innovative quilt designs based on a single design concept.

Published and distributed by

Nancy Dill, QuiltWoman.com,

info@quiltwoman.com

Copyright, Cary Flanagan, 2009

"After the Storm"

The Story of Hannah Applegate Benson Stone

First Edition, Archway Publishing Company

Copyright, Cary Flanagan, April 2016

Second Edition,

Copyright, Cary Flanagan, May 2021

Publisher:

"Your first family is your blood family and you'll always be true to that. That means something. But there's another family and that's the kind you go out and find. Maybe even by accident sometimes. And they're as much blood as your first family. Maybe more so, because they don't have to look out for you, and they don't have to love you. They choose to."

Dennis Lehane

Harold Harvey

This book is dedicated to:

to my 'found' family of friends.

I thank you for being part of my life!

Acknowledgements:

Many people helped me in developing my story, researching 19th century Arizona, reading early drafts, editing my manuscript, and creating beautiful artwork. To each of the following people I owe a debt of gratitude!

Jill Hough, Arizona Historical Society, Flagstaff, AZ for invaluable information about life in and around Flagstaff, circa 1900. Specifically, attitudes towards and between White, Hispanic, and Native populations; attitudes towards women choosing to divorce, remarry or remain single, but in a relationship; types of ranching in the area at that time and what life would have been like on a ranch; possible legal outcomes for domestic abuse and attempted homicide.

Kathryn Dodson, (Next Step Book Coach), who spent hours reading and editing my early drafts and helping me to prepare for publishing and marketing my finished novel. Your help has been invaluable. I am grateful for your knowledge and encouragement.

Caroline Macon Fleischer, Editor, (Reedsy) developmental editing of an early draft of my book. You helped shape and clarify my story. Thank you for your insights and encouragement.

For reading later drafts and offering feedback and constructive criticism, I thank **Cathy Bowen, Edie Hartshorne, and Kathryn Leblanc.** I deeply appreciate your contributions to this book.

Ashley Santoro, Artist, (Reedsy), for outstanding cover design and artwork. It was fun working with you, and I look forward to future collaborations.

My deepest thanks and appreciation go to **my husband Ron,** for putting up with me for many months while I have been involved with research, writing, and rewriting – so much that he often had to make dinner and clean the kitchen for me! I love you.

"We do not receive wisdom; we must discover it for ourselves, after a journey that no one can take for us or spare us."

Marcel Proust

PART I

June 1898 – July 1898

Chapter One: June 1898

My stomach churned. I dug my fingernails into the palm of my hands to try to make it stop. "Please," I said softly, "please don't let me throw up!" I couldn't sleep a wink the night before and had too many butterflies in my stomach to eat any breakfast this morning knowing what I was about to do.

It was one of those mornings that could not make up its mind: blue sky with scudding clouds one minute, making way for sullen gray skies the next. Just when you thought rain would start, the sun would break through again. There was a light breeze, and it felt cool for June. It was the kind of day Mama liked to call 'fidgety.' *Oh, Mama.* My heart lurched along with my stomach.

And there we were, standing stiffly together while we waited for the train to pull in, Mama, Ben, my little sister Becky who had insisted on coming, James looking handsome and dapper in his brown tweed traveling suit and bowler hat, and me. I had purchased my gray traveling suit just for this trip, but I felt strange wearing it, as if it had been made for somebody else.

My plain straw hat perched awkwardly on the pile of my blond hair. I did not know what to do with my hands.

Ben reached out to James to shake his hand. James shook it but evaded Ben's eyes.

"Where are your parents or other members of your family?" Ben asked. "Didn't they want to meet your fiancée and see you off?"

"They did not want to make the trip over from Tamworth," James said. "We said our goodbyes at the house. And besides, I think they are happy to see me gone."

Ben looked surprised but did not pursue the question as we heard the train approaching in the distance. "Take good care of my daughter," Ben said, with a pained expression. James nodded but said nothing. Mama had a handkerchief to her eyes. Becky had grabbed my hand and did not want to let go.

"Please, Sarah," she said. "Please don't go." I gave her hand a squeeze and smiled at her. There really was no more to say. I looked briefly at James and he gave me a tight smile. Sunlight crept between the clouds at that moment, but the air around us chilled me.

Finally, we heard the whistle of the train and the chugging sounds as it rolled slowly to a stop. While passengers stepped off the train around us, we hastily said our goodbyes. Mama gave me a tight hug and whispered, "I pray the lord keeps you safe and brings you back to us someday. I love you." Tears ran down her cheeks, and I gave her a quick kiss as I turned away.

I could not look directly at Ben, but I mumbled, "Take care of her and keep her safe." James tipped his hat to Mama and Ben, then he helped me lift our valises and picnic basket onto the train.

I did not dare look back. The expression of wrenching pain in Mama's eyes almost pulled me back down the steep iron steps. However, I was resolute. I had made my stand against my mother and stepfather. I had chosen to go with James, a man my parents did not know, and who I knew only from stolen moments when I was able to sneak away from home to meet him in secret. I adored him. He was so handsome and said the sweetest things to me, and when he touched my hand or kissed me, he set my heart aflutter and made my body burn. Now, I held my head high and stifled my desire for one last look at Mama's distraught face and my fear of the future I had so rashly chosen.

Earlier that week, in the beautiful drawing room of our spacious home, the home that Ben had so lovingly designed and built himself. Mama had called me an angry, thoughtless child during our last quarrel. I didn't care. I was leaving my childhood behind in the small New Hampshire village where I grew up in my search for a new life. I felt very grown up at seventeen and knew what I wanted.

"Please think carefully before you make any hasty decisions," Mama had implored.

"We have already made up our minds."

Ben said "I forbid you to go. We do not know this man!"

"You are not my father," I spat at Ben. "There is nothing you can do. I have made up my mind." I saw him recoil as if he had been physically struck as I whirled out of the room. I had a momentary flash of guilt at hurting my parents, especially Ben–he had always been kind to me. But in that moment, it did not matter.

That was just a few days before James and I boarded the train with only a few possessions, our youthful idealism and sense of adventure to sustain us.

Chapter Two

Once I settled in my seat beside the man I adored, my courage began to ebb. I turned my head towards the window to hide my tears. So many emotions buffeted me. The train rocked and shuddered, gaining speed. We passed along the west side of the lake I had gazed at from my bedroom window as a little girl, and soon we were in unfamiliar surroundings. I had never been beyond the confines of our small town, and now–now this train carried us towards the Great Unknown in the Arizona Territories. Suddenly it was more than I could bear, and a sob escaped me.

James immediately put his arm around my shoulder and pulled me close.

"What is it, dearest?" His words were tender, but I was ashamed of giving way like a baby when we were just starting our great adventure. I hastily dried my eyes and smiled at him.

"It is nothing, James. Only a little sadness over leaving home". I did not add my fear that I might never see my Mama or my family again, especially my beloved brother Jacob, who had refused to see me off at the station. "I am truly happy to be here with you." I placed my hand on his arm and squeezed affectionately, then I leaned against him and buried my face in his chest. The dark tweed of his coat was soft.

I slept for a while, nestled against James's warm body, feeling safe for the moment. Later, when I sat up again, I laid my hand gently over my soft belly. There was nothing to feel there yet, but there would be soon enough. It was my secret—not even James knew. I would send word home once we were safely married. There was still time.

The gentle rocking and creaking noises of the train were soothing, and I began to relax. We were almost all the way to Boston, passing through farmland and small towns that reminded me of my own hometown. It was afternoon already, and my stomach growled with hunger. We decided to eat some of the provisions that Sallie Mae, our cook, had packed for us in the large basket: fruit, sandwiches, half a roasted chicken, and fresh-baked cookies—a feast! James noticed an envelope under the napkin at the bottom of the basket and pulled it out.

"Here, you open it," he said. "It must be from your parents." Inside the envelope, I found a note from Mama and Ben and $100.00 in small bills.

"Lordy, look at all that money", James said with glee. "That should be enough to get us by until we get to the Territories and I can find a job! Your parents sure are generous. My Pa gave me what he could, which wasn't much."

I was more interested in the note. In Mama's careful handwriting, she wished us both well and hoped we would have a safe journey.

"More important than anything else, my dearest Sarah," she wrote, *"is to remember how much Ben and I love you, how much we all love you. I hope you and James will make a good life together but know that we will miss you more than you can know. I pray we will see you again someday.*

Please let us know how you are and where you decide to settle."

"Your loving Mother, Hannah"

Tears began to well up in my eyes again, but I hastily brushed them away. I handed James the note.

When we reached the train station in Boston, the enormous size of the place and the noise overwhelmed me. I had never seen anything so grand, nor had I ever seen so many people, some hurrying about, some sitting on hard wooden benches, surrounded by their baggage and sometimes by fussing children who were anxious and tired.

James spotted a ticket booth, and we went over to get our tickets, thankful we did not have much to carry. I stood to one side while James spoke to the ticket master. The man behind the ticket counter asked James if the tickets to Chicago and then to Flagstaff were for a round trip. I could see the excitement on James's face when he said, emphatically, "No! One way only!" It sounded almost like a boast.

My heart pounded. *We are really going to do it. Maybe never come back.* I felt my stomach threaten to heave for a moment, then I steadied myself.

On our way to Chicago, we sat on hard wooden seats on the left side of the train car. They were uncomfortable and made my bottom numb. I had plenty of time to think about our future and what I was leaving behind. My mother had been my rock and primary support when I was younger. Leaving my brother Jacob hurt the most. I adored him. He had always been my closest friend when I was growing up. He had tried vehemently to talk me out of going, but I was un-swayed. I was excited about leaving, I had been daydreaming of this this day for many weeks. I believed James and I could create the close-knit family I wanted so badly. Now I was not so sure I had made the right decision. What in the world have I done?

I knew so little of James. He was the youngest of three, with much older brothers. They grew up in Tamworth about ten miles west of my village. His family raised horses and cut timber. He never spoke of his parents or any other relatives. He had few if any friends. That was most of what I knew. When I asked for more information about his family or what it was like for him growing up, he either said nothing or said he did not like to talk about it. "Enough of these questions," he said sharply, once. I did not want to anger the man I loved so much, so I stopped asking.

I tried to conjure up an image of my father, but all I could come up with was my mother's description of how he had looked, as a young man, and how he had been killed in an accident logging with his brothers. I was only two when it happened. No memories of him came to me. Instead, I had only the vague sense of something missing in the months following his death, when my mother was as remote as if she had not been there at all. Since that time, I'd felt an emptiness inside me, an absence that needed to be filled. I hoped that James could fill that space.

Then images of my brother Jacob came to mind. My playmate, my friend, I could always count on him when my world seemed uncertain. We had played endless games of hide and seek in the woods around our cabin and giggled in our beds at night, up in the loft, when he told me funny stories. We were inseparable. But after Papa's accident, he, too, had withdrawn for many months and rarely played with me, even when I begged. They left me totally alone. And now it is me that is leaving.

In my earliest memories, Mama is standing in the kitchen in her apron, her hands covered with flour but her eyes far away. I would wrap my arms around her legs and beg to be picked up. I was perhaps three. She would absently pat my head and tell me "not now," leaving a large floury handprint in my hair. Sometimes when we were in the garden together, weeding, I would ask her questions, but she would ignore me, too preoccupied to answer.

When I was older and she started paying attention to us again, her fierce love for Jacob and me was comforting, but it was also confusing. I remembered the times she read stories to me or helped me to make a dress for my doll or explained how the seasons came and went on our farm. She taught me how to care for the chickens, goats, and the cow. And I helped her brush Molly, her mare, and fill Molly's feed pouch.

Sometimes I helped Mama in the kitchen, peeling potatoes or shucking corn for dinner. She showed me how to make piecrust and fill it with sliced apples in the fall. I delighted in having her full attention during those special times. But even when she was with me, she was often only half there. It was rare that she could do only one thing at a time. She always had a task in hand, some mending, or kneading bread, for example, to occupy part of her attention when we were together. She never stopped long enough to see the hurt inside me, and I never lost the feeling of emptiness and abandonment I felt during the time of her greatest grief.

Mama never talked of my father. There was an unspoken rule that Jacob and I were not to ask questions about him. Such questions were too hard for her to bear.

Then, just when life started to seem normal again, a terrible storm raged for days and destroyed much of our farm. I remembered how scared Jacob and I were and how our mother tried to calm us and to keep us safe. Despite her own fear, she kept us warm and fed and tried to keep away the darkness.

Then we met Ben, and everything changed.

Ben brought a breath of fresh air into our family. He had arrived unannounced to help with rebuilding and repairs after the great storm toppled trees and seriously damaged our farm buildings and home. Papa's brothers also came to help with the devastation, but they were no match for Ben.

A big bear of a man, strong, with seemingly

endless energy, Ben was gentle with Jacob and me and told us wonderful stories of growing up on a farm in Canada. We all fell in love with him. I was happy when he and Mama decided to marry. I was six. Jacob was eight. Jacob liked him too but was wary of him as well. I wanted to call him Papa after the wedding, but Jacob said he was not our Papa and I should call him by his name. I still felt Mama's love and how she cared for Jacob and me, but our family quickly expanded, and Mama's love eventually stretched to encompass four more sweet babies. Our closeness was never the same after that.

I was seven when the first baby was born. I was amazed by how tiny she was and her funny little scrunched up face. Mama allowed me to hold the baby briefly and the infant smiled and gurgled in my arms. I was smitten. How could I love anything more? During the years that followed another adorable baby arrived every couple of years, another girl, then a boy, and another girl.

The first, Becky, was named for Mama's beloved aunt Rebecca, who raised her. Lyddie, was named for two of Mama's closest childhood friends, Lydia, and Jane; Bennie was, of course, named for his father, and Maggie was simply Margaret Abigail for no other reason than they liked the name. I loved each child as she or he arrived.

I grew up changing diapers and playing with infants and rambunctious toddlers. Mama taught me the basics of sewing when I had time, and of course, I went to school during the day with Jacob, to the same one room schoolhouse my mother had attended as a child. I loved to read, but most of my time at home was taken up with the care of the little ones while my mother designed and made quilts. Mama was never really mine again, but I was a good girl, always helpful, and always waiting for my own life to start.

I recalled Ben's bear hugs, his devotion to Mama and hers to him, and how he was besotted with each new baby in turn. He professed to adore Jacob and me as much he did his own children, but was that real? Did he really mean it?

As I grew older, I tried to fit in to this new family, but I resented the loss of closeness with Mama that I still longed for as each new baby arrived. I became caretaker of each new infant and "nanny" to the older ones. I loved them all, doting on each wee babe as she or he arrived, but I still felt resentment as well.

After Maggie was born, my parents hired a Nanny/Housekeeper. I was no longer a caretaker, no longer needed. Was I still me? Did Mama still love me for myself? I no longer knew my role in the family. I felt like I was adrift.

Now I had James. Will I be able to count on him in the same way I counted on Jacob? I thought back to the time when we first met at the Farmer's Market in our village the previous June. He had asked me to dance with him that magic evening and to walk in the moonlight with him afterwards. He was so handsome. His bright eyes and warm embraces were enticing. We saw each other often after that. My feet floated off the ground wherever I went.

In warm weather, James would ride over from Tamworth on his beautiful black gelding. Sometimes we would spend a few hours before dusk rowing around Silver Lake, near my parent's house. There were many inlets where we could 'disappear' and talk. Sometimes we took a picnic into the nearby woods and would lie together in the soft pine needles. Once he let me ride in front of him on his horse and we galloped along the back roads. I loved feeling his strong arms around me. I loved everything about him.

When he asked to meet me secretly, sometimes during the day, when I skipped school, or in the evening when we could more easily hide ourselves, I could not say no. The sweetness of his words, the feel of his kisses, the electrifying touch of his hands on my body in the stolen moments we could find now and then, his murmured words of endearment and encouragement. I was only sixteen. What did I know of love? His words filled my heart and eased the emptiness inside me. I was powerless to resist him.

One time, Jacob told my parents that I had been skipping school and that he thought I was meeting someone. My parents confronted me, to ask how I could be meeting someone behind their backs. I had never seen Mama so angry, and Ben was pacing back and forth, trying unsuccessfully to control his temper. He scared me a little.

"How dare you meet some young man we do not know anything about in secret and skip school to do so?" Mama fumed.

I lied, of course, and then felt terrible about lying. All I wanted was James—I could think of nothing else. Nothing else mattered.

Back when we lived on the farm, I wanted nothing more than to live out my days there, maybe marry and have children, but to live with the rhythm of the seasons on the farm that my father had begun to create. When my mother married Ben and our family moved, first to a cramped house in Conway, then into the large, elegant home Ben designed and built back in the village, I hated the large home and all it symbolized. It was too big, too fancy, too luxurious. I yearned for the simplicity of the farm. I did not feel like I belonged there.

I had loved the farm, the quiet of the woods and fields, the gentle patterns of daily life, with everyone responsible for doing their part to keep our lives moving along in a natural way. There were no servants to wait on us, no one to make our lives easier.

When I met James, as he began to tell me of his dreams of going out west and working on a ranch, I fell into his dream. I loved the idea of a new life somewhere else, free from my childhood and my family. I had no idea what life on a ranch would be like, but it had to better than this.

The train jerked me out of my reverie. We were pulling into another small community and people were waiting on the platform ahead and I was struck by a terrible realization: I could not remember James ever asking me directly to come with him and be married. I just assumed that was what he meant. And here I was, embarking on an enormous adventure into the unknown, and carrying a new life under my heart! I don't care–Everything will be alright! I am so crazy about James that whatever happens is meant to be. I shut my mind off any other thought.

Chapter Three

When James and I settled as best we could into our uncomfortable seats for the night, he kissed me and held me close, and I snuggled against him. "Sleep well", he said into my ear "Only one more day to endure on this cursed train before we get to Chicago."

I slept fitfully, with images of home, Mama's stricken face, and my siblings' voices begging me to stay interrupting my sleep. When morning came, I made my way as quickly as I could to the lavatory at the end of the car, where I was thoroughly sick. When I felt a bit better, I returned to the seats that James and I shared. Thankfully, James did not seem to notice, although I am sure I did not look my best. We ate what little was left of the food from the day before.

The terminal in Chicago was even more grand than the one in Boston. It had enormous green marble columns, and the same marble covered all the floors. There were large stained-glass windows which brightened the space and a ceiling which seemed to go on forever. I had never seen anything that approached this magnificence. And there were people everywhere–

so many people, hurrying this way and that. I saw faces of every color from coal black to light brown, as well as white, and every race I could imagine. It was like a large cooking pot with many colors and flavors together. A distinguished-looking gentleman stood near us. He had a long white beard and was wearing a white robe and a turban. A young Black woman was dressed in the height of fashion, wearing a beautiful feather-plumed hat to match her outfit. She pushed an elaborate wicker carriage holding an infant swathed in fancy linens. Her husband walked beside her dressed in a smart suit and wearing a top hat. I hardly knew what to make of it all.

Six tracks left this station under an amazing overhead structure made of glass, so it took some time to find our train. Fortunately, we found more comfortable seating this time. I was exhausted by the time we settled but James found us sandwiches and drinks to take with us. I felt better once we had eaten. We settled into a comfortable sleeper compartment – what a luxury after our previous experience.

I had brought a book with me to read, the recently published and much talked about "The Awakening", by Kate Chopin. It had apparently shocked many readers when it was published, but the story intrigued me. It is about a young contemporary woman in an arranged marriage in a society which gives her no room to make a life of her own beyond that of wife and mother. Women of her social status give themselves to their husbands, in all ways and everything they own becomes the property of their husband. She has no independence and needs his permission to do anything outside of their home. This aspect of the story shocked me as well, although I had heard that women give up much when they marry.

The heroine feels suffocated and unloved in this arrangement and eventually has a love affair. That must be what is so shocking about this story. It simply is not done. I did not yet know how the story ended, but it seemed clear that this arrangement could only end badly.

I put the book down and gazed out the window at the endless passing fields, farms, small villages, more fields and rolling hills. The book got me thinking. What will I be giving up, to marry James? I did not want to even think about that, I was so besotted with the idea of being his wife.

For his part James was restless and bored. He spent some time walking up and down the long corridor of our car and he soon made friends with a group of men a few compartments forward. They played cards to pass the time and invited James to join them. I could hear the low murmur of their voices and an occasional laugh or loud exclamation, as someone won a hand. I was happy for him.

When James returned to our compartment, his face was flushed. He avoided my eyes. "Did you enjoy playing with your new acquaintances?" I asked him.

"It was OK," he said, evasively. "They seem nice enough. They are going all the way to Flagstaff too. Playing cards with them will give me something to do along the way. They also say they know the area around Flagstaff and might know someone who is hiring when we get there."

"Where are they from", I asked, hoping to learn more about these men.

"They didn't share much about themselves." James said. "They were mostly just interested in playing cards. They did tell me their first names. Charlie is in his fifties, I would guess. The others are likely in their thirties or forties. I think they came from back east somewhere. Like I said, they seemed friendly but not very talkative. I sure hope they can help me find a ranching job" He laughed. "They said I did not look much like a wrangler, but I told them I had grown up around horses and thought I could handle the work. That was about all the talking we did."

I was glad James had found some distraction for our long journey, but something in his tone made me feel uneasy. He did not offer to introduce me to his new acquaintances.

When we stopped at a larger town to let off passengers and pick-up new ones, we got off the train for a few minutes to stretch our legs and get a breath of fresh air, for which I was grateful. Vendors gathered on the station platform and we bought sandwiches and drinks. After one of these stops, I decided to check the money in the envelope Ben and Mama had given us for the trip. The train tickets had cost more than I expected, and the food as well. We had already spent more than half the money we started with. I made a mental note of the amount that was left and decided we would need to be more frugal if there had to be enough for lodging and food in Flagstaff until James could find work. I resolved to check the envelope again before we reached Flagstaff.

Eventually we entered the mountains of the Great Divide. Magnificent, jagged peaks covered in snow surrounded us, even in springtime. Nothing back home had prepared me for such grandeur. I was amazed and humbled as the train brought us over rugged high passes and down into steep valleys. I marveled also at how the rail lines could have been built in such rugged and difficult conditions. I had heard that many men had been lost in the building of the railways.

After a particularly fitful night with little sleep, I made up my mind to tell James about the baby. I was nervous. He would find out soon enough and I preferred the news came directly from me. I prayed he would be happy.

As we sat together after an unappetizing breakfast, I broached the subject.

"James, I have been thinking. I would like to get married as soon as we get to Flagstaff."

"What's the hurry?" James said. "I have to find a job and we should settle somewhere before we think about marrying. No one knows us in the Territories, so it will not matter if we pass ourselves off as a honeymooning couple."

"Well, I have a reason not to delay our wedding." I paused, gathering my courage. "I know you would prefer to wait until we are settled, but there is something I must tell you." My voice shook as I said, "We are going to have a baby!"

James looked shocked, and I saw him struggle to cover his feelings. "Well, dearest, that IS good news!"

He said the words, but the look in his eyes and his voice told a different story. He clenched his fists.

"James, I know the timing is all wrong, but just think, a new little being will be here this winter. I do hope you will be happy." I put my hand on his arm and whispered, "Please, James. This will be **our** child, together, a symbol of our love."

I heard him swear under his breath, "a symbol of our love, indeed. How the h—l did this happen?" But to me, he gave a weak smile. "As you say, my dear, we must be married right away."

"I thought you wanted to get married and have a family," I said, near tears.

"Yes, eventually," he hissed at me. "Not now!"

He got up abruptly and went down the aisle of the train towards his card playing companions. I did not see him again until late that evening. I was already in bed when he came into our compartment.

"I am sorry I was so cross with you earlier. It was just such unexpected news! We will manage somehow." He kissed me and fell asleep immediately. I could smell alcohol on his breath.

Chapter Four

After what felt like weeks but was only a few days, we arrived in Flagstaff. I looked around me with wonder when we got down from the train. Everywhere I looked, I saw tall pines unlike any with which I was familiar back east, and sharp mountain peaks covered with snow beyond. The sun was bright and warm on my skin, and the air was dry and crisp. The fresh air revived me after the endless hours on the train. I skipped a little, as I turned in every direction to see this new and marvelous place!

"Oh, James! How wonderful it is here! Look at those mountains–have you ever seen the like? What a beautiful place to begin our new life together!" He wrapped me in his arms and kissed my cheek.

"Yes, it is," he murmured.

Then the magic began to fade a bit, as I noted deeply rutted dirt roads in all directions, and dust rising with the passing of men on horseback and a buckboard wagon or two. The buildings nearby were unpainted and dirty, except for a few imposing buildings made of red stone, newly built nearby. It was a strange mix.

Thankfully, it was just a few steps to a small hotel next to the train station, and we headed straight for it.

James's new friend Charlie was headed in the same direction.

"Let's celebrate our arrival with a few drinks," he suggested. "And we could play a hand or two." My heart sank a little. I wanted James all to myself for our first night together in a real bedroom. Thankfully, James said "Not tonight. Let's meet tomorrow after we are rested". They agreed to meet at the hotel at noon the following day.

The hotel had a wide verandah in front, as well as a balcony overhead at the second level, with wood posts and carved wood 'gingerbread' where the posts met the next level. It reminded me of the wide verandah and decorative details on the house I had grown up in. There was a double door for the entrance with a large, stained glass window gracing each side. The lobby seemed welcoming if a bit shabby.

While James arranged for our lodging at the imposing entrance desk, I immediately asked for a bath to be brought up to our room. I had been wearing the same outfit since I left home and could not wait to get out of my soiled clothes and soak in a tub of hot soapy water.

Our room was on the third floor of the hotel, overlooking the main square of the small town. The room was plainly furnished but comfortable enough for someone who was beyond exhaustion. I collapsed onto the soft bed and was almost asleep when James appeared with our bags. I jumped up, embarrassed, when a young woman entered the room carrying a copper bathtub and another woman lugging a large pitcher of boiling water. This she poured deftly into the tub and added the pitcher of water from the washstand. She handed me a small bar of soap and a towel.

"Will this do?" she asked, "or will you require additional hot water? That will cost another 50 cents to carry up".

James gave her a small tip and said, "that will do for tonight. Thank you. Tomorrow we will need our clothes laundered and another, larger bath prepared before dinner."

"Yes sir", the woman said and left.

I entered the steaming water and sank into it in sheer pleasure, while James busied himself unpacking. I took my time soaking and washing. At length I rose and dried myself and donned my one clean nightgown. When I entered the soft bed, I fell immediately asleep.

I stirred sometime later when James came to me, the sweet smell of the soapy bath still lingering on his body. I felt his hands on my breasts, his need hard between my legs and his mouth on mine.

"I love you so much", he whispered. "We are finally almost home." I awakened enough to welcome him, and we made sweet love together for the first time in a new land. Then I slept hard and undreaming, the stress and exhaustion of our trip slipping away.

When at last I awoke the next morning, James was already up and dressed. He had gone downstairs to request breakfast be sent up to our room, and presently we heard a knock at the door. The same young woman who had brought our bath water the night before stood in the doorway with a tray holding a coffee pot, mugs, toast, and jam. James tipped her and she gave him a pretty curtsy.

I felt like a queen, sitting up in bed, sipping my coffee, the first real coffee we had had since the beginning of our journey, and eating the thick slices of delicious, toasted bread covered with strawberry preserves. My, what a luxury!

"James", I said, nervously, "how can we afford such a fancy room and breakfast? How will we live until you find work and a place to settle?"

"Don't worry about it, sweetheart," he said, grinning. "I figure we deserve a bit of a honeymoon, even if we are not married yet. I have a little cash I have been holding out just for this time and besides, I want to treat you special while I can. You can be sure we will not be able to do this again once we are living on a ranch. And besides, it is your birthday! I bet you thought I would forget."

He drew a small package out of his pocket. In the small box were two gold rings.

"This one was my grandmother's. It is for our wedding. My mother gave it to me just before we left." It was a lovely plain band with an inscription inside. Sarah read the tiny script: 'May Love Abide.' "This other one is just for you from me." He showed me a ring with a lovely red garnet in a simple gold setting. The stone sparkled in the light of the kerosene lamp. It was beautiful.

"Happy birthday, my beautiful almost bride".

"Oh, James. I can't believe you are really mine and that we are about to marry! How in the world did I get so lucky?"

"From the moment I first saw you across the crowd at the market festival, I knew you were the one for me. You were and are so beautiful! I am the lucky one."

I smiled up at him, overcome with feeling, and he leaned over and kissed me. Then I was in his arms again.

"Now that you are truly mine and we do not have to sneak around in haylofts anymore, I just can't get enough of you", he said against my ear.

"Nor I you", I whispered back, barely able to speak.

Afterwards, James dressed again and told me he was going out to meet his friends and begin his search for work and a place for us to live. I washed in the basin (thanks to an additional pitcher of water brought up by one of the young women) and put on my remaining clean chemise and dress. I determined to take care of having our traveling clothes cleaned and pressed while James was gone, and then I would venture out to see what I could of the town.

Chapter Five

About two o'clock that afternoon, James returned to the hotel, his cheeks flushed red with excitement.

"Charlie says there is a ranch southeast of here, a pretty big one. Charlie knows the owner, and it just happens he is in town for a couple of days to get supplies and do some business. His name is Patrick McBride, and Charlie spoke to him about us. He has invited us to have an early dinner with him tomorrow night. If all goes as I hope, he will take us out to the ranch the following morning! What luck, I declare!"

He picked me up and swung me around, forgetting we were in the hotel lobby. I blushed scarlet as I saw several people looking at us. Thankfully, they were smiling.

"Oh James, how wonderful! But what will I wear? I only have my traveling outfit and this one. And we must be married. And…"

James said, "do not worry about it, dear one. I learned of a shop nearby where we can get you a new dress and hat for this special occasion. I will get a new coat for myself, as well. Perhaps a new shirt or boots. We can go there now if you like."

"But how can we afford such a luxury, James," I blurted out, thinking of the amount of money left in my parent's envelope.

"I was lucky at cards," he responded with a grin. "Very lucky. My new friends did not know I was such an accomplished poker player!" I turned my face away. The thought of the happiest day of my life being paid for with gambling money annoyed me. Perhaps once James is working on the ranch full time, he won't have time for such games.

"That would be lovely, James. I would be delighted to look for a new dress and hat for our wedding and this auspicious dinner." I said the words, but I was not happy.

We walked along a rough wooden boardwalk in front of a row of shops and saloons until we reached a side street. Dried mud and deep ruts ran between this walkway and another on the opposite side of the street. Wagons and men on horseback plodded along, and a stagecoach stopped at the hotel where we were staying. I did not see many women among the groups of people walking or riding in the streets, and the men wore mostly rough clothing. I was nervous, walking beside James who still wore his traveling clothes.

We turned right and found another, similar but narrower street and board walk. Soon we came to a shop with a sign in the window that said, "Purveyor of Fine Clothing for Gentlemen and Ladies and Other Sundry Items." When we stepped inside, I was struck with a familiar smell: I was reminded of Great Aunt Rebecca's sewing room at home. I had to catch my breath before I could look around. My heart ached a little.

A young woman approached us. She was tall and graceful, with auburn hair piled on top of her head in the current style. Her long dress was a pretty shade of dark blue with a high neck and long sleeves of dark blue lace, which complemented her pale skin. Behind her another woman was busy arranging one of the shelves of fabric. She was quite striking with lovely red curls around her face and over her shoulders, pulled back with a pretty ribbon that matched her pale peach dress. It was a wonderful combination.

"Welcome", the tall woman said to us, extending her hand to first me and then James. "My friends call me Blue. This is my friend and business partner Grace."

Grace came forward and extended her hand. She said, with a laugh, "My friends call me Grace." A beautiful black cat wound around her feet and stretched luxuriantly as she spoke. It had long silky hair and golden eyes. "This is Amber", Grace said, bending over to stroke the cat and pick her up.

I liked them both immediately, and somehow, felt they were people I could trust.

"I need a new dress, something nice enough for a small wedding ceremony but not too fancy", I said, blushing. "A dress that I can continue to wear later for special occasions."

"And I need a new shirt and suit jacket," James

interjected. "For the same wedding," he said with a grin.

"I know just the thing for each of you," Blue said. "Is the wedding yours?" At my smile of assent, she said, "Then I wish you both all happiness for the rest of your days together! Come this way." Gesturing, she continued, "When is the wedding?"

With some embarrassment, I said, "Tomorrow, if possible. We will be leaving Flagstaff day-after-tomorrow to start our new life together."

"Hmmm", Blue said, looking at each of us with some curiosity. "Usually, a dress takes several days to make, with your choice of fabric. But perhaps we can find something suitable already made as a sample. I can probably adjust the fit, if necessary."

We followed her past several racks of dresses in the center of the room and a wall filled with shelves holding all manner of fabrics to our left. It made my head spin, and I felt a pang of homesickness rise within me. The smell and the many dresses reminded me of my Great Aunt Rebecca and her dress shop. I had spent hours in her sewing studio and shop as a child.

Blue pointed to a display of dresses. "Look at these. Do any of them strike your fancy?"

There were six or seven dresses in front of me, in various shades of pale rose or a soft caramel. They were perhaps a year or two behind the current fashion, but I didn't care. They were lovely.

"May I try on this one?" I asked, holding up a soft

cream cotton blouse and matching skirt with white lace cascading over the bosom of the blouse and down the front. The high neck and long sleeves were also of lace.

"Of course, my dear. That color suits you perfectly with your blond hair. And later I can make some adjustments, so it is suitable for everyday wear. Come this way, we have a private dressing room. If you need any assistance, let me know."

Meanwhile, Grace helped James find what he needed. It was not long before he had chosen a handsome pale beige shirt, brown wool jacket and a dark string tie. When I emerged from the dressing room. We were both amazed at our mutual transformations.

"Oh, James," I said, "you look so handsome! All you need now is a proper hat and a walking stick!"

"And you, my dear," he responded, "You are a vision! Turn around so I can see all of you!"

I twirled and admired myself in a long mirror. "How fortunate the dress fits without alterations. I have never worn a dress as beautiful as this one! But can we afford all this, James? This dress costs $10.00! I have never had to buy a dress, since my mother or Aunt Rebecca made all our clothes. This seems so extravagant."

"Hush," James said. "Remember, I told you I have been lucky. We have enough to keep us for a while. I am going to go down the street to the church and see if I can find the preacher to arrange for our wedding tomorrow." He thanked Grace for her assistance, paid for our purchases, kissed me on the cheek, and left.

"Oh Blue, I am so happy. I am the luckiest girl in the world! Will you come tomorrow and stand up for me at my wedding? We have only just arrived in Flagstaff and know no one. That is, except for some gentlemen James met on the train. I would so love to have a woman friend by my side! Or two women," I said looking at Grace.

Grace smiled and said she would leave the honor to Blue. "Someone needs to stay in the shop. Blue will make a lovely Maid of Honor."

"It would be my pleasure," Blue said. "But where are your parents, your family and friends?"

"I left them behind, in New England," I said shyly. "James and I want to make a new life for ourselves here. It is a long story. It will have to wait until another day."

"Just let me know what time tomorrow and I will be there for you. I will dress your beautiful hair for you too if you like. Perhaps a new hat to go with your ensemble? I have just the thing to go with your dress!"

"Would it be possible to borrow the hat for the day? I will not need such finery where we are going." Blue assented and said she could bring it back to her shop later in the day.

I floated back to the hotel, where I met James a while later. "It has all been arranged. We will meet the preacher at his home. Charlie and Frank will stand up with us."

"How lovely," I said. "And Blue has offered to

stand up for me. It is perfect! Perhaps we can invite them all to have a light supper with us at the hotel."

Chapter Six

The following day, as arranged, James and I dressed and made our way to the preacher's home. We could have had a church wedding, but under the circumstances we decided this was fine for us. The preacher met us at the door. He was spare and white-haired but had a kindly look. Presently his wife joined us as a witness. She was of similar age, plumpish, with a round face and friendly eyes. Charlie and Blue joined us a few minutes later. Frank did not appear, and Charlie had no explanation, but did not seem concerned. Blue had picked a few wildflowers and gave them to me to hold. I was touched.

James and I held hands as the preacher spoke his words over us, and James slipped his grandmother's ring onto my finger. Before we knew it, we were husband and wife! I felt giddy with happiness. We thanked everyone there and invited them to come to the hotel for a toast and some refreshments. James and I led the way down the street with the others following. A few people stared, but I hardly noticed. My eyes were only for James.

A short time later, after James had stood everyone to a toast and the hotel had kindly offered some small refreshment on the house, Blue pulled me aside.

"Sarah," she said in a low voice, "Flagstaff is a rough town with many temptations. Gambling halls, saloons, fast women. I don't want to alarm you, but I have met Charlie and several of his friends. Just be careful."

I did not want to hear or comprehend her words, but I was grateful for her offer of friendship. I squeezed her hand and thanked her. She kissed me lightly on the cheek. How little I knew at that moment how much I would need her friendship.

After a passionate night with James and a deep and dreamless sleep, we awoke to a bright and sunny day. We enjoyed another wonderful and lazy breakfast in our room, then decided to take a little tour of Flagstaff and the surrounding area, hiring a small wagon, horse, and driver to take us around.

Flagstaff, as we soon learned from our guide, was small but growing. The 'downtown' consisted of only four or five blocks, but already contained a busy train station, two hotels, a few shops, a bank, and numerous saloons. A large brick edifice stood two blocks from the center. It was apparently the courthouse for northern Arizona. Beyond the central area, more imposing buildings were under construction, as well as homes. Our guide told us lumber, sheep herding, and cattle ranching were the foundation of Flagstaff's development.

The roads were still very rough, but one could easily see the vision that had been established for the town. I was thrilled that we would be starting our new lives together as part of the establishment of a new and developing community. Everything I had dreamed of, all those weeks and months ago was coming to fruition–a handsome and loving new husband and the exciting prospect of a life working on a ranch, just as we had wanted. How did I get so lucky?

Chapter Seven

That evening, at 6:30 pm, as instructed, we met the owner of the Copper Stallion Ranch at a hotel several blocks west of the hotel where we were staying. I wore my beautiful new dress but put a shawl around my shoulders to lessen the effect a bit. James wore his elegant outfit from the day before. We stepped carefully along the boardwalk to get there.

The Mountain View hotel looked a bit newer and more modern than our hotel. A restaurant and bar were off to the right as we entered. Seated near the fireplace in the center of the room was a tall man with dark auburn hair and mustache, with well-muscled arms and shoulders. He smiled and gestured to us to join him.

"Patrick McBride," he said, stretching out his large hand, first to James and then to me. He lifted mine to his lips and gave the back of my hand a light kiss. "I am pleased to meet you, Mr. Parker," he said warmly, "and your lovely bride. Congratulations on your nuptials! Please, join me for dinner. We can talk about what I have to offer you."

Dinner consisted of grilled beef ribs, Mexican fried beans, fresh salsa and sour cream, and roasted potatoes. There was a variety of fruits for dessert. It was a wonderful feast, except for the salsa, which, for me but a bit too hot. Mr. McBride and James drank several beers, but I declined. The two of them seemed to be sympatico, for which I was grateful.

"Please tell us about your ranch and its beautiful name?" James asked.

Mr. McBride said "Many years ago, as a young man, I came here to work on the railroad. Like a lot of young men of the time, I had dreams of working on a ranch someday. I learned how to ride and eventually I earned enough money to leave the railroad. I set out to find my future.

"I met up with a group of wranglers and captured and tamed a wild stallion. He was the color of polished copper, beautiful and intelligent. Eventually he became my constant and most loyal companion. He is the sire or grandsire of many of the horses on the ranch. I decided when I bought the property, to name the place after him. I purchased a small house and barns and 500 acres of land about 20 years ago and have expanded much since then. Copper left us just a few years ago. I miss him every day."

"How big is the ranch now?" James asked.

"About 1,000 acres, give or take. Earlier this year, several of my hands took off to join the soldiers fighting the war down in Cuba. I guess they thought soldiering would be more exciting than working cattle. None of them ever came back, so, meeting you is my lucky day!" He gave a hearty laugh. I was struck by how welcoming Mr. McBride was and how willing to take a chance on strangers from way back east.

"You have a lovely accent, Mr. McBride," I said. "It reminds me of a woman I know back home who came over from Ireland not too long ago." James raised an eyebrow in question.

"I am Irish. You have a good ear," he said. "My grandfather came to this country with two of his brothers, about forty years ago. They settled near Boston, in Massachusetts. My grandfather met his wife there and they raised a large family. They did quite well with a small produce business that grew over the years. My father was the youngest and he became interested in the expansion of the railroads through the central and western states and territories. He and my mother moved to Omaha, Nebraska where the first rails of the Union Pacific heading west were laid. Apparently, I inherited his love of trains and moved out here before I was twenty to be part of bringing the eastern and westerns sections of the railroad together. It was an exciting time, but I was a much younger man then," he said with a laugh.

We discussed the terms for James's employment and mine. "I grew up as a wrangler of horses," James said. "My family raised and sold horses all over New England. I am sure I could learn to wrangle cattle in no time."

Patrick asked how I would feel about being the caretaker of a large flock of chickens and developing a vegetable garden, large enough to feed everyone on the ranch. I was thrilled with this prospect and said so.

"I grew up on a small farm and am experienced in caring for farm animals and gardening," I said. "I always preferred living on the farm to living in town. This sounds perfect for me. Thank you!" I said with enthusiasm.

In exchange, there would be a place for us to live, provisions, and a monthly cash stipend for each of us. James and I both agreed to the terms.

Early the next morning, with no more lolling in bed to enjoy a fancy breakfast, we set off with our small store of worldly goods with Mr. McBride in a well-used wagon drawn by a mule. With the back of the wagon loaded with bags of potatoes, flour, dried beans, and all types of feed for horses, cattle, chickens, and menfolk, we took off on our new adventure. James and I sat up front to drive, while Mr. McBride led the way with a fancy team and fully laden wagon ahead of us.

We left Flagstaff through a thicket of scrubby pines. After that, all I could see through the fields of tall grass that seemed to fan out beyond us for miles was the narrow track made by the endless passing of wagon wheels. After what felt like hours, I finally spied ahead of us a large red barn and a similar but smaller house off to the left. A stand of pines stood tall behind the buildings, and the white tips of mountain peaks made an imposing backdrop behind them.

We were approaching our destination and our future. I stifled my need to vomit.

PART II

July 1898 – November 1900

Chapter Eight

When we first arrived at the ranch, all that existed of our future home was a large hencoop and a shed up a small hill away from the barn and house. The shed appeared to be in rough shape. There were gaps between many of the boards making up the walls of the shed, and there were gaping holes in the roof. The whole structure tilted to one side. I was horrified. How are we going to live in that?

The hencoop, too, needed a lot of work – there were holes in the wire fencing where the chickens could get out and predators get in. Chickens ran everywhere around the grassy area near their roost.

"James – what are we going to do?" I was in tears, too exhausted emotionally to think clearly. This was never part of my dream.

"Wait and see," he said to me. "It will be fine. After all, there was no way for anyone to know that hiring a new hand would include a wife. We can't very well live together in the barn with the other hands." But I could see the annoyance on his face. This is not what either of signed on for!

A short time later, I met with Cora McBride in her large and attractive kitchen. It smelled of baking bread and the preparations for dinner.

"I know seeing your new home may be a shock for you and your new husband, but I can assure you we will have it fixed up for you two in no time. It was such an unexpected and pleasant surprise that Patrick would hire a married couple and I am so happy to make your acquaintance!"

She offered to let James and me sleep in their ranch house until we could have a decent place of our own. She said "We have an extra room we mostly use for storage. There is a mattress and bedframe and bedding you can use while you are here and take with you when your cabin is ready to move in. There is also a small table you can have with two sturdy chairs. Once you are settled, we can see what else you may need."

"You are too kind. How can we repay you?"

"Tending these neglected chickens and supplying us with eggs is all I ask of you. And eventually a vegetable garden," she said. "And, of course, your husband's help with the cattle and horses."

An unexpected sob escaped me before I could stop it.

"Oh, now, child. Don't you worry none about your new home. Patrick and the boys will fix it up, just fine for you. The hencoop too. It will be comfortable and cozy in no time! I can help you get settled after the men are finished if you like." I could find no adequate words and simply smiled in gratitude.

When I first met Cora, I was struck right away with her warmth and her welcoming manner. She had likely been quite beautiful once and still had a striking profile. She was taller than I was and looked like she had spent much time working out of doors. Her skin was deeply tanned, and her dark blond hair was just beginning to turn silver in wisps around her face. She plaited it in a heavy braid down her back. She wore a white blouse embroidered with flowers and a long skirt that I could see was split like pants so she could ride horseback.

"Please call me Cora, I don't like to be formal. And I want you to meet my children. My eldest is Julia," she said, gesturing to a slender girl with long wavy auburn hair. "She is fifteen and quite the accomplished young lady. Paddy, named after his father, is twelve and is learning to be a horseman and to rope." He had not begun to reach his height, but I could see he would be strongly built like his father. "Sammy is eight and is learning how to take care of the calves and horses, and little Katie, who is five, is learning to love animals of all kinds, especially kittens! We have a new litter if you would like one when you are settled. Their mother is a terrific mouser."

Each child, as she or he was introduced, held out a hand to me with a genuine smile. The girls even gave me a little curtsey. I could see that Auburn and blond hair ran in the family, not to mention freckles. What adorable children! Such nice manners. Cora asked them to call me Miss Sarah, which made me feel proud and grown up.

"Do they go to school?" I asked. "Or are you teaching them at home? I have wondered what children living on ranches do to learn to read and write and the other things that are important for children to know about."

"I have taught my children the basics and we go into town to the library every few weeks and spend several hours there each time. We always bring home stacks of books that are suitable for their ages and interests and we all learn together, even me! My youngest, Katie here, adores reading. She has been able to read since she was three! Such a smart girl!" Cora gave Katie an affectionate hug. "We all try to spend part of each day, usually after dinner, reading aloud to each other and talking about the story or the subject of each book."

"That's wonderful," I said. "I would love to see the books they like. Thank you for telling me about the library. I love to read also, perhaps I could come with you the next time you go? I would like to sign up to be a member."

"I would be happy to have you join us next time if you are available. The children love our outings and have learned a lot from the books we borrow. I am sure they would enjoy your company. The library is quite small still, just one room. I don't know what we will do when we have read all the books they have there!" Cora and the children laughed at that.

I felt at ease with Cora from the beginning. How lucky we are to have found this living situation and such kind employers. And what lovely children! And that amazing skirt!! I determined I would get a skirt like hers and I could not wait to go horseback riding. The image of old Molly entered my thoughts. My mother raised her from a filly, and I remembered her as an affectionate mare who allowed me to ride her bareback when I was a child, with my mother holding her lead. *Mama…*

Our first night in the McBride ranch house was awkward. James and I wanted to be close but did not want to disturb anyone. We made love as quietly as we could and thanked our lucky stars and the good Lord that we had arrived at this wonderful place.

I was surprised by the size of the ranch house. On the outside, a wide verandah wrapped around two sides of the house, which was painted the same red as the large barn. However, the house itself did not appear overly spacious. But once inside, I discovered that it had been added onto several times at the back, to accommodate a growing family. I learned that the girls shared a bedroom, as did the boys, with Mr. and Mrs. McBride occupying a third. Another room used mostly for storage, became a guest room on rare occasions. That is where James and I slept for several nights. A large kitchen and family gathering room completed the home. It was bright with light from many windows and heated by a coal stove at one end, in addition to the cast iron cookstove at the other end. A large table with a long bench on each side filled one entire wall of the kitchen.

The morning of our first day on the ranch, James met his fellow ranch hands while I assisted Cora in her kitchen with cooking dinner for everyone. Cora did most of the work while I watched or handed her ingredients as she asked for them. I finally got up the courage to tell her I had no idea how to cook.

"I am embarrassed to tell you, Cora, I have never had to prepare a meal in my life!".

"Gracious, girl. How did you grow up and never learn to cook?" She was amused. "How about I give you some lessons so you can feed your new husband when you move into your cabin?"

"Oh, that would be wonderful," I said. "I would be much obliged."

"We will start tomorrow. Since you will be staying here while your cabin is built it will be convenient. I will show you breakfast basics, then dinners, then we will move on to bread and biscuits. We don't eat fancy here, but we are well fed. When we get to know each other better," Cora continued, "I would like to hear about where you and James come from and how it happened you grew up not knowing how to cook." She smiled warmly at me when she saw me blush in my embarrassment. "Never you mind, child. We will teach you everything you don't already know!"

"That sounds perfect. Thank you so much." My face must be crimson!

In addition to Cora and Patrick McBride and their children, there were six "cowboys" who worked for the family along with two of their wives and children and a few grandchildren. It was a lot to take in at first, but everyone seemed friendly enough and welcomed us to their "family". The custom was for the hands who stayed in the barn to gather at the ranch-house for breakfast and dinner. James and I would join in these meals until we could move into our own place. The married hands lived on the outskirts of the ranch in their own homes and ate at home with their families, while the rest bunked in a part of the barn that had been fitted out for them. Clay and Fletcher lived with their families about five miles north-east of the ranch house, while Luke, Lorenzo and two other hands I had not met yet lived in the barn.

The men offered to help us turn the dilapidated shed into a decent home. They found a supply of salvage lumber in the barn with which to enlarge the shed and build a second room for our bedroom. They brought hay and straw bales from the barn to pile up against the outside walls on the north and west sides against the winter winds. They added double layers of boards with straw in between for the bedroom.

"The winters here can be brutal," Luke said. "It is the wind that does it, blowing across these open fields. It will help when you can get a stove to heat the space. We are making it as tight as we can." I was grateful for the insulation and their extra care.

Between the cabin and the chicken coop we found an old root cellar, dug about four feet deep and roughly four feet wide by five feet long. It was filled with dirt and weeds and the remains of dried-up vegetables. I would need to clean it out and enlarge it before it could be used.

Behind the house the men dug a deep hole and

constructed a rough outhouse, the "necessary", we called it. There were a few off-color jokes that I heard during construction when the men thought I was out of earshot.

Not much like my old home, surely. In all the time I was dreaming about our new adventure in an unknown setting, I had never imagined a place like this, and it had somehow not occurred to me that, as a wife, I would be solely responsible for many household tasks that I had never encountered before.

As a young girl, I had lived on a small farm in a simple cabin. After my mother remarried, we eventually moved to a rather grand house with six bedrooms, large dining and drawing rooms and an indoor bathroom with hot and cold running water. There was also an enormous kitchen with a well filled pantry and a cook! We had a housekeeper/nanny to look after the house and four rambunctious children while my mother was busy building her mail order business as a quilt pattern designer.

And now, we would be living in a shed.

Oh my! What have I done? I felt a wave of panic. I am no longer a young girl filled with dreams and idealism, but a housewife responsible for keeping our house and preparing for a baby. I have never even cooked a full meal before or been required to do laundry or clean up my room. What kind of life will I be bringing my baby into?

I made up my mind to love my very first home with James, do what I must. I kept my feelings to myself. There was plenty of time to create the home of my dreams, if that was still what I wanted. It would be nice to have another room and maybe a verandah like the one on the ranch house. But for now, this would be perfect.

Chapter Nine

The house was not much yet, but already I could visualize how I wanted it to look inside. I would ask James to purchase a cooking stove on his next trip to Flagstaff. I would ask Blue for fabric to make curtains for the windows, and, of course, we would need bedding for James and me and a crib or basket for the little one who was on her way. (For some reason I felt sure I was carrying a girl child.)

Perhaps Blue would allow me to use her sewing machine to make the things we would need. The sewing lessons Mama gave me may be helpful, after all.

There was a small flock of chickens already, about a dozen layers, but no one had been taking care of them consistently and they looked half-starved. Mr. McBride asked James to go back into town to purchase another dozen hens, a rooster, and enough feed to keep them until spring. I asked James if I could come with him to get what I needed from Blue.

"We can find out about ordering the cook stove as well, and lighting of some kind. We will be needing the heat soon enough."

A few days later, when the cabin was almost finished, James and I took the same wagon we had arrived in and made the trip back to Flagstaff. This time it did not feel quite so far, but still it took more than two hours to get there with the mule. It seemed different from when we were there before, somehow, but only because we came into town a different way. There was a general store on the main road about a half mile west of the town center where we had first stayed. You could purchase almost anything there and it reminded me of the general store back home. We could get provisions there as well as chicken feed. We were able to put the chicken feed (for eight months) on the McBride account as well as most of what we would need ourselves over the summer and for the winter, (bags of onions, potatoes, flour, apples, and sugar), including a kerosene lantern and lamp, along with a large can of kerosene.

It turned out we could even order our cook stove there! The proprietor showed us pictures of several different models to pick from. How convenient! The one we chose was cast iron like the one my parents had but not as big. It had six burners on the top, a small oven and separate tank to heat water. Two small round shelves perched above the cooktop for keeping things hot, like coffee. The oven door had the word "Romantic" emblazoned across it. It seemed meant to be. We agreed to pay half when the stove arrived and would ask Mr. McBride if he could help with the remainder. We would have to spend our entire monthly stipend. It was a gamble. There was only a small amount of money left from James's gambling.

Then the proprietor, Mr. Freeman, said we should consider having a gun or two out where we would be living.

"You will be isolated–perhaps the missus should have a rifle against an occasional wild cat or bear. Or perhaps a handgun, just to be safe." James considered this, and against my wishes, purchased one of each.

"You are going to need to learn how to shoot," he said to me sternly. I did not respond.

"There is a farmer not far from here who might be willing to sell some chickens," Mr. Freeman, told James. "Just go west out of town a couple of miles. You will see a sign for Windy Mountain Farm, "Fresh Eggs". James agreed to drop me off at Blue's shop and said he would meet me later when he had the chickens.

I was so happy to see Blue and Grace! It had only been a few weeks, but I had really missed them. They were happy to see me as well and each gave me a warm embrace. Fortunately, they had no customers at that moment and Blue was working in the backroom, making a new dress for a client. She made us a pot of tea.

"My mother taught me to sew on a machine very similar to yours," I said. "Yours is beautiful and more modern. Mama is an amazing quilter. She is also a professional quilt designer and pattern maker! Her proudest possession is the sewing machine my father gave her when they were first married. When our house burned down years later, her sewing machine was the first thing that she wanted to save, after the children and animals, of course!"

"How lucky for her she was able to save it and your family. I can see where you may have gotten some of your spirit," Grace said.

"I think I have seen some of your mother's quilt patterns," Blue said. "Doesn't she have a mail order business?"

"Yes! Yes, she does! Where did you see her patterns? It is hard to believe they have made it all the way out here! How amazing!"

Blue said, "I saw them in Denver recently when I went to visit some relatives of my father. I was also on a buying mission for the shop. Your mother's patterns are wonderful. I will make sure to order some, now that I can say I know the daughter of the designer! Perhaps I can even make some samples. You must be proud of her."

I winced. "Yes. But she is part of the reason I left home. My family is large, and my mother is busy with her business and her younger children. I felt like it was time for me to find my own way, especially after they hired someone to look after the children and take care of the house. There was nothing for me to do! It was almost like I was being edged out of my own life! I am grateful to have found James and a wonderful situation on the McBride's ranch."

"I am sorry to hear about that, but happy you ended up here! I just know we will be good friends."

"Tell me about how you and Grace came to own

this store. I have not seen many women yet in Flagstaff. It is comforting to know there are women like you nearby and not just the ladies in the saloons." Grace and Blue exchanged a look and smiled. Then Grace extended her hand to Blue's face and moved some hair away from her eyes. It was a remarkably tender gesture.

Blue said, "My pa came to Flagstaff with my mother in the early days of the town, from St. Louis. He came for the lumbering operations. Flagstaff then was just a few businesses, a bank, several saloons, and, of course, the train station. It was a rough place, and she was a city girl. I don't think my mother was happy here There was mud everywhere most of the year when it was not covered in snow!

"Pa did very well and moved up to management in the lumber company he worked for. He eventually built a grand house for the family. Sadly, my mother died giving birth to me before she could enjoy the new house. Pa raised me, with the help of his neighbors, Grace's parents. Grace became my closest friend when we were children, and after Pa died when I was about eighteen, Grace and I decided to live together in the house that Pa left to me. In addition to the house, I inherited enough money to purchase this business so I could support myself. That is the short version of our story–I will tell you more another time."

We were silent for a few minutes. Then I changed the subject by telling them why I was there. "In addition to seeing you, of course, I do need some fabric for curtains, bedding, and items for a baby. I am also going to need some new clothes. What I brought from home is not suitable for ranch work. One thing I would like especially is a divided skirt so I can sit astride a horse, though, of course, it may be some months until I can safely ride. I will also need loose clothing for when my baby makes me grow bigger." I blushed. "Can you help me?"

"Congratulations!" said Grace. "Of course, we can, just wait and see! How far along are you now?"

"Probably about two and a half months," I said.

"Then there is plenty of time to gather what we need for when your baby comes. The other items, such as curtains, bedding, and some of the clothes you want we can get for you sooner." Blue measured me, with Grace recording the information as well as details for the curtains and the bedding I would need.

James came for me shortly after that, and I told him we would need to return soon, to pick up what Blue would have ready for us. The next day James taught me to shoot a gun. There were predators and who knew what kind of human vermin were around, he told me. He took down the rifle he had mounted above our front door.

"This is how you hold a rifle," (he held it in shooting position so I could clearly see where my hands should go and how to balance the gun). "And this is how you put the bullets in." I nodded. I was feeling annoyed by his assumption that I did not know anything about guns and decided not to let on that my mother had been a great shot with a rifle when I was growing up and had taught me how to shoot at an early age. It had certainly been a while, but I figured I could remember how a rifle worked.

We went outside. James had set up a row of bottles on a log at some distance away from the cabin. I took up the rifle and put the bullets in, just the way James taught me and made a show of trying to figure out how to hold it.

"Ok. See those bottles over there? I want you to aim the gun and when you are ready, fire at the one at the left."

I did. The bottle exploded.

"Very good!" James said, surprised. "Try hitting another one."

In a flash, six bottles exploded.

James looked at me with his mouth open. "Where did you learn to shoot like that?"

"My mother taught me," I said, grinning and pleased with myself. "Do you want to see what else I can do?"

"No!" James said and retreated to our cabin. He was quiet when I served dinner that night. I was quite proud of myself.

Chapter Ten

I began developing a garden area to the east of the chicken coop. It would need to be quite large to feed our family and all the hands on the ranch. I was excited to start this major undertaking. When I lived on the small farm my father carved out of a dense forest, my mother, Jacob, and I took care of the farm after he was killed. The happiest days of my childhood were preparing the garden every spring, planting, cultivating, then harvesting in the fall. It became a kind of ritual between my mother and me.

After my mother married Ben, we lived on the farm in the summer, continuing the cycle of planting and harvest. Then we moved into town for the winters. I hated living in town, even though it was more comfortable. Undertaking this new garden project felt a bit like coming home.

I said to Mr. McBride, "I think we can feed everyone on the ranch if the soil and water conditions cooperate. I will need extra help to get the ground ready now and again next spring and summer with planting and weeding."

"Please call me Patrick." Mr. McBride said, "I do not want us to be so formal."

One blessing was that a small seasonal stream cut through the property and came close enough to the chicken house, garden, and our new home for us to dig an irrigation ditch which could supply some of our water needs, at least after the summer monsoon rains and until we could get a proper well dug.

I asked James to get some of the hands to help dig the garden, considering it would help to provide some of their food. James was not very enthusiastic, but because of my condition, I was able to persuade him to recruit Luke and Clay to help. They got permission from Patrick to set aside a couple of days from their regular work to get the garden ready.

I could see an area that had once been a garden but was long since grown over. I wanted a larger area. I paced off about 40 feet and put a stake in the corner. I then paced off 30 feet perpendicular to that and put another stake. James brought some twine from the barn and we staked out thirty feet by forty feet on all four sides. I decided that was enough to start with.

I asked James and the other men to begin along the outside lines to dig and then turn over the grass so that the roots stood up in the air. The grass was long and the roots deep in the soil. It was a huge job, but they tackled it with energy. I was amazed at the color of the soil when it was turned up – it was dark and as red as rust. About half-way through they stopped for the day. They finished the next day and began cutting a channel from the stream to the edge of the garden.

The men built a large wooden tub where the channel brought water to the garden. It could hold enough water so that we could easily gather pails full when needed, except in the dry season. It saved a lot of time and effort from carrying water from the stream itself, for which I was grateful, but I looked forward to the time when we would have a real well close to the house.

The next step was fertilizer for the garden. The old hay/straw/manure from the horse stalls had been sitting for several years in a large pile behind the barn. Luke and James took a wagon and filled it with this horse manure and brought several loads up to our new garden. Once they had been dumped, the men spread the manure across the entire garden. Then soil from the old chicken coop made ideal topsoil for the new garden. What a huge accomplishment! I was so appreciative of everyone who helped!

We were a sight, dripping wet with sweat and dirt. I wished heartily for a proper bath. Clay spoke up, wiping his face with a dirty rag.

"Did you know there is a nice little swimming spot on the stream over yonder?"

"No. Where?" James asked. "Can you take us there? I sure could use a wash and cool off.".

"Sure, follow me." Clay said and he, James and Luke saddled up and headed off towards the stream.

"Hey? What about me?" I shouted after them. James circled back.

"It wouldn't be ladylike for you to be there with us. And besides, you can't swim," James said.

"I most certainly can swim," I shouted after him. "I grew up being able to swim!"

"Well, you can't come with us. You can wash yourself and your clothes in the ditch water." He trotted away after his friends.

I was so mad I could spit nails. After rinsing off the worst of the dust and dirt and pouring buckets of water over my long hair, it occurred to me I might just be in the right frame of mind to kill a chicken. I had been dreading having to do that for a while now, but I was angry enough to kill a bull with my bare hands.

I went into the chicken coop and selected the oldest of our layers. I had watched as my mother had wielded an ax over a chicken's neck as a child and had helped with the plucking but had never had the nerve to do this myself. However, I was resolute, as well as angry. WHAM! This is part of being a responsible adult, after all. I wish James could see just how ladylike I am now!

I set up the firewood and coal for a good fire in our outdoor cooking pit and made a wonderful stew, trying not to think about the chicken I had killed. I filled a large pot with water, the cut parts of the chicken, mixed with cut up potatoes, carrots and onions and some savory herbs I had "borrowed" from Cora, and hung the pot on the frame James had set up over the fire. I let it simmer for several hours. I had half a mind not to let James have any for dinner, but I relented. He said he liked it. It was the first time I had ever cooked a whole chicken stew, and I was quite proud of myself.

The next morning James surprised me by staying in bed longer than usual. He sat beside me in bed, looking sheepish.

"I want to apologize to you for yesterday," he said. "I know you have been working hard, especially in your condition, and you deserve better. I understand why you were so annoyed with me. What can I do to make this up to you?"

This pronouncement was so unexpected I hardly knew what to say.

"James, thank you for saying that. Indeed, I was more than annoyed. You are lucky you got any dinner at all last night!" He raised his eyebrows at that but did not comment. "Honestly, there are many ways you could help me, especially in the coming months. The water bucket is feeling heavier and heavier. Soon it will be a strain to carry it from the new holding tub all the way to the kitchen. Not to mention, the coal bucket."

"I can help with that before I go down to the barn in the morning. I will just get up a little bit earlier. Speaking of which, I had better get going." He got dressed, then gave me a kiss on my cheek. "I will try to get home earlier tonight."

Oh my, he really does love me.

Chapter Eleven

One day, when I was hauling water to the house, it struck me that a good water supply way out here on the ranch could be difficult to achieve in dry years and not always reliable even when there was adequate rain. Cora had recently explained some of the local weather patterns to me. Apparently, July and August were the usual months for rains, which were called monsoons in the Territory. You could count on a thunderstorm and rain most days in summer in a good year. When they did not come drought was inevitable. And it has not rained for the past two weeks. Our makeshift irrigation trench would need to be supplemented by a well before the next growing season.

Patrick had a deep well with easy access to both the house and the barn. It had a lid across the top to keep sand and debris out of the water and a roof. A hand pump attached to a long pipe was set in the center. A bucket sat nearby. Patrick had installed a large metal tank that could be kept filled for the horses and cattle when there was not enough water in the stream for their needs and the men used it to wash off the worst of the dust each day.

I asked him about the possibility of digging a well near our cabin.

"That seems a bit unlikely," Patrick said. "Your place is up the hill a-ways. A well would have to be very deep to reach the water table. Another idea is to build a holding tank of some kind. If it's built right, it could be filled by snow run-off in the spring, and again when the rains come in the summer."

"You mean something like a catch basin?"

"Exactly," said Patrick. "We can dig out an area like a small pond, banking the dirt we dig out along the sides, then line the whole thing with rocks and cement. If we shape it right, water from snow melt will be guided towards the holding tank. What do you think?"

"Sounds like a lot of work, but worth it in the end. Cora told me the last few years have been dryer than usual. It will be a major project like preparing the garden, but I am willing to help, if the others are up for it."

"Good," said Patrick. "I will map out a likely spot and talk to the men. My friend at the General Store can help with materials and suggestions, I would guess. We will want it completed before the ground freezes and the snows come."

My home in New Hampshire, with indoor hot and cold running water at the turn of a faucet, is looking mighty tempting right about now! I am feeling like a real pioneer!

By this time, it was already well into July, too late to plant most vegetables, but Cora gave me some seed to try for sunflowers and various greens. In a shady area I tried lettuce, spinach, Kale, and chard, to see what might grow in this heat. I was rewarded eventually with greens for our table for a few weeks, and the chickens would be delighted with the Sunflower heads come fall.

Meanwhile, of course, my belly grew larger, although not so large that I could not still hide it under my skirt. When I visited Cora in her kitchen a few weeks later, she gave me a perceptive look.

"I notice you are growing a bit rounder. Are you carrying a little secret under your apron?" She laughed at her own little joke. When I blushed and nodded, she asked, more seriously "How far along are you?"

"I think about four months, maybe a bit more" I said.

"Hmmm," she said, counting on her fingers. "A mid-winter-birth. We will need to prepare. I have birthed four children and helped birth several others. I will come to you when you are ready. Meanwhile, let me know if you need anything."

"Thank you. I am grateful, and my mind is eased knowing I will have assistance when my time comes.

"I do have an unrelated question. I am curious

about one of the hands–Luke. He was so helpful when I expanded my garden. It was almost like he could do the work of two men. He looks different from the others What can you tell me about him?"

"Luke is mixed blood. I know little of his background, only that he showed up here one day when he was about fourteen or fifteen, riding a pony bareback, and looking pretty much starved. He said he needed work and he looked it. We decided to take a chance on him, and he has proved to be one of our best wranglers. Patrick and I are fond of him and I would trust him with my life."

I had to admit, Luke intrigued me. I determined I would learn more about him when the time was right.

You know how animals prepare their nests, salvaging twigs, or straw, or leaves – whatever they can find to make a soft nest for their babies? I did the same, gathering feathers from the chickens and clean straw. I had been given a large basket by Clay's wife, Martha, in which I layered these materials and topped them with a soft blanket that Mary, Fletcher's wife, had given me. I set the new bed next to mine. I was nesting.

Chapter Twelve

The loud clatter of horses' hooves and wagon wheels broke the silence one morning after James had left for the barn. I ran out to see what was making so much noise, and there was our new cast iron cook stove on the back of a well-used wagon! I felt like a little child on Christmas morning and clapped my hands with glee.

"Oh, how wonderful," I said, as the driver climbed off the wagon seat. "It is surely getting cold in the early mornings and nothing to warm us up."

The man said his name was Johnson and he was from the general store in Flagstaff.

"This here stove just came on a late afternoon freight train yesterday. I got it out here as fast as I could." Mr. Johnson was wearing dirty coveralls and an old wool jacket. He was tall but did not look strong enough to move the stove anywhere.

"Looks like you will need some help getting this off the wagon and into the house. My husband and the other men are either in the barn or nearby. I will go fetch them."

"That would be a great help, ma'am. This thing weighs near a ton." He laughed.

I followed the path down to the barn while Mr. Johnson untied the ropes holding the stove. When I got to the barn, I could hear voices.

"James, Luke, is anyone here?" I called. Luke arrived right away, followed by Fletcher. James arrived soon after.

"What's up, Mrs. Parker?" asked Luke. I had long since asked the men to call me Sarah, but some of them still insisted on being formal.

"Our cast-iron stove has finally arrived. We need help getting it unloaded and into the house. Can any of you come?" I was grateful that all three of them came with me. In a few minutes, they were hauling and heaving the stove to the ground. At length, with groans and a few colorful words, the stove was in place in my small kitchen. Then they connected it to the stovepipe that had been installed when the back wall was completed. All that was left was to unload a small supply of coal to get us started. We would need to get a wagon load or two soon to keep us through the winter. Just in time for much cooler weather. I am so grateful for the stove. Now we can be comfortable, and I can make hot meals for a change. Maybe I can even learn some of the finer points of baking!

In September preparations began for the annual running of the cattle up to the train lines just east of Flagstaff. The drive would not commence until October, but there was a lot to do to prepare.

None of that involved me, of course, but it meant James was gone from early morning until sunset. He would arrive home for dinner, exhausted and ravenous. I made sure to have a hearty dinner waiting for him, and after eating he generally fell into bed, with virtually no conversation between us.

Of course, I wanted to spend more time with James but, to my surprise, it was a relief for me. I knew he preferred talking with the other hands down at the barn to conversing with me, and I was not particularly interested in hearing about his day on the range. Instead, I savored the quiet. I had plenty of preparations to take care of myself. There were vegetables from the garden to put up for the winter and root vegetables and potatoes to safely stow in the root cellar. There were the onions and garlic bulbs to braid and hang to dry, and the herbs that Cora had given me from her own herb garden to hang as well.

I took great pleasure in these tasks–they reminded me of the harvest times with my mother at our farm when I was growing up. It was an annual ritual that she and I enjoyed together. I enjoyed being alone now to enjoy this special time. I am thinking of you, Mama, and missing this time with you. Do you remember that time when we were picking the last of the corn and a skunk came to visit us? And that flock of wild turkeys who came to gorge on what was left in the garden after harvest?

A large celebration would follow the end of the drive–a feast for the hard-working men to look forward to. I had promised two roasting chickens as my contribution. I was glad we had allowed more than a dozen eggs to hatch during the summer, so we had plenty of young chicks for the coming year.

The day before the big feast, I steeled myself for the killing and prepared the hens for roasting. I put carrots, garlic, onions, and potatoes in the pans surrounding the fowl, and cooked them in my small oven one at a time. The smells from them roasting was heavenly, and I was sorely tempted to eat some.

Early in the morning of the appointed day, James was out of the house after a hasty breakfast. Soon, there was a great noise from the corals behind the barn, with Patrick McBride leading the hands, on horseback beside and behind the cattle. Several herding dogs surrounded the throng of animals as they helped guide them north to the rail yards.

The noise of the cattle, the yelling of the cowboys, the excited shrieking of the children watching, and the barking of the dogs was deafening, while a cloud of dust from the cattle and horses plumed over the ranch. I watched from the safety of my cabin. In the afternoon, I carried a heavy basket with the dinner I had prepared down to Cora's kitchen. She had prepared refried beans, tortillas, large bowls of fresh salsa and several other mouth-watering dishes. There would also be steaks and ribs added to the big outdoor grill just before dinner. This would be such a treat from our usual daily fare of rice, beans, and vegetables, sometimes with cheese and salsa for a change but rarely any meat.

The men straggled back later than expected. Apparently, they had decided to celebrate at one of the saloons in Flagstaff and were quite inebriated when they returned. Still, they enjoyed the feast we had prepared. I had to help James's back to our cabin later that evening, where he fell into bed and was immediately asleep.

Chapter Thirteen

Work began in earnest soon after the cattle run, to dig the catch basin Patrick had planned to help ease our periodic water shortages. Since the workload for the men had been lightened with all the mature stock gone, they were able to devote a few hours every day to digging out what would amount to a temporary pond, about sixteen feet wide by eighteen feet long and about four feet deep at the lower end. It was a huge undertaking, but everyone recognized the need, and were rewarded at the end of the day with several beers.

With seven men the work went more quickly than we had thought it would. I even helped a little by packing down the earth that was thrown up onto the sides and in piles fanning out from the top edges of the pond with a piece of board. I tired easily, and Patrick told me not to strain myself. But I enjoyed being part of the work crew. It gave me a chance to get to know the men better.

Patrick went into town to get the supplies needed to seal the inside of the basin and we all spent two days covering the bottom and sides with cement. That was a very messy job but fun. After a few weeks we were able to test the seal and it held We were finished!

We decided to have an informal party to celebrate our accomplishment. Once again, great food, beer, and some fiddle music. What fun! I wish we could do this more often!

Luke approached me while I was standing at a table serving food. It was the first time I had seen him up close and the first time I had seen him all cleaned up. Even his hair was washed. I was struck again by his unusual features. Oh, my, what do I do now? I could feel myself flush.

"I hear this big dig was your idea," Luke said to me.

"Not really. I wanted to dig a well near our cabin, but Patrick said that would be too difficult because of its location. It was really his idea, but we talked about the plan together".

Luke gave me a wink and said, "I think you just like to see the men working hard."

I laughed but just then caught James's eye. He looked annoyed. I quickly walked over to him.

"I am so impressed with how hard you and the others have been working to get this project finished!" I said to him.

"What were you and Luke talking about?", he said. His tone was cold.

"Nothing important. We were just talking about

how happy we were that all the hard work was done, and we could all celebrate. That's all."

"I don't like you getting too friendly with the men," he said gruffly. I was put out by what he said but kept it to myself. Later that night, I found myself fuming. What right does he have to tell me who I can be friendly with and talk to? I don't want a marriage where I must ask my husband's permission to do anything like the wife in that novel I read.

I determined I would have to talk to James about that. I would have to think carefully about how to say what I wanted to say.

The next night, when James came home, I had a delicious dinner ready for him of chicken stew with lots of vegetables in it. It had been simmering over the fire all day and the aroma was heavenly. James was surprised but pleased by this special treat.

"What is the occasion?" he asked. "We had a party last night, so it can't be another celebration."

"I just wanted to do something nice for you," I said. "For us, actually. I have been wanting to talk to you about some things." I ladled stew into two bowls and handed the larger portion to him.

"I see. What things?"

"Well, for instance, what you said to me last night, after I had a brief conversation with Luke."

"That I do not want you getting friendly with the hands?"

"Yes. Last night Luke came over to me to say hello and to talk about the new water tank project. It would have been rude of me not to talk to him." I paused, searching for the words. "What I really want to say is that I resent being told who I can talk to."

James stopped eating. "Is that right?"

"James, I am a grown woman. I may be only eighteen, but I don't appreciate being treated like a child. If someone wants to speak to me, I will respond, regardless of who it is. Are you telling me you have a list of people I am not allowed to talk to?"

"No, no. I don't. Just Luke, I guess."

"Why Luke?"

"I see the way he looks at you. I see the way he flirts with you. I don't want him near you."

"James, Luke is nothing to me. I should not even have to explain that to you. How can you be jealous when I am growing bigger with your child every day?"

"You are right, my dear. I am sorry. Let's say no more about it."

However, I heard an edge in his voice and he turned his back on me when we retired to bed.

Chapter Fourteen

By mid-December I was beginning to feel unbalanced, and it was difficult to stand for any length of time. Of course, I still had the chickens to feed and eggs to look for, some of them hidden in strange places. Not to mention keeping our stove going with heavy buckets of coal.

James was no help. Despite his promise of a few months ago, he kept away as much as he could, telling me he had chores and responsibilities at the barn. He was with me in early morning after sleeping with his back to me all night. He returned for dinner, but that was all. At least he had agreed to take over one of my responsibilities—taking a basket of eggs to the ranch house every day or two.

I don't understand why he has no interest in the birth of our child—his child. And what happened to his promise to help me as my time came closer? It hurts me so much! Sometimes I could not help the tears that fell when he left in the morning.

Light snow had begun to fall every day or two,

leaving just a few inches of powdery white. Soon, snow was a daily occurrence, though still not heavy. I began to worry that no one would be able to get through when I needed help.

One afternoon I heard a soft knocking on the cabin door. Cora had come to see me and to assess my needs. She had arrived on snowshoes and we agreed there needed to be better access for when it was my time.

"I will speak to the men about clearing a path from the ranch house to the barn and from there to your door."

We had a pleasant visit. We talked about some of the books she and her children had picked out on their recent trip to the library. I had wanted to go but did not feel comfortable going as I was.

"Cora, it is so nice having you here! I have been cooped up for too long without company. It gets lonely, sometimes."

"I understand how you feel. It is not easy in winter to get around, especially in your condition." She handed me a well-worn cowbell. "Ring this if you need any assistance. The sound carries a long way. I also have a tea I want you to take. It will make you more comfortable in your final weeks. It is an old family recipe containing herbs for relaxation. You are young and this is your first, so we must be watchful. I will visit with you again soon. Remember–ring the cowbell if you need anything!"

"My mother bore four babies when I was younger,

and I helped a little. I remember what I need to have on hand—clean sheets, boiling water, a sharp knife. Is there anything else I should know?"

"Sounds like you are better prepared than I thought you would be. We will have time to talk about details later."

James arrived home for dinner just then. He nodded to Cora. I could smell alcohol on his breath.

"Cora.is going to help me birth our child. She has had lots of practice, apparently."

"That's fine," James said, slurring his words. He muttered something unintelligible and went into the other room while I made dinner. He did not reappear until morning.

A few days later several of the men, including Luke, but not James, beat a path to our door on snowshoes and promised to keep the path open when it snowed. Luke knocked on my door to say hello, along with Lorenzo.

"I so appreciate your help, both of you. I am feeling a bit isolated up here," I said to them.

Luke said, "If there is something we can do for you, or anything you need, let us know."

"Thank you, Luke. But it would be best for you not to come here when James is not at home. I hope you understand."

"I see," Luke said. "We are only trying to help." I

heard an edge in his voice.

"I know. And I appreciate that, but James may not. That is all I able say. Thanks again for your help."

Chapter Fifteen

A few days before Christmas, the McBride family invited us and all the hands and their wives to join them for a Christmas feast. The children were also invited, and the adults were encouraged to bring a gift for one of the many children who would be there.

"What can we bring?" I said. "We have so little." But then I thought we could bring cookies. I remembered the wonderful sweets our cook Sallie Mae used to make for the holidays, though I had no idea how to make them. Cora's tutorials had not included cookies, and I gave up on that idea. Oh well - no cookies this Christmas! Of course, I could provide a couple of chickens for roasting.

Christmas morning came very cold and crisp. When the sun rose, it seemed all the world was made of diamonds. Light sparkled off the crystals in all directions. It was magical.

As soon as I got the fire going in our stove and made the coffee, I tended to the chickens. They were snug in their roosts with only a few eggs to gather, but they seemed glad of the feed I put down for them. I had killed and plucked two chickens the day before, and this morning I rose early to dress and roast them. They were well seasoned with garlic and herbs, and the smell coming from the oven made me hungry.

We all gathered at the McBride ranch house about noon. I dressed up as well as I could with a long blouse hanging over the top of my skirt and a warm shawl. James wore his wedding suit. He walked confidently in front of me while I gingerly made my way down the snowy path. What a blessing that Luke had done such a good job clearing the pathway, with no help from James.

When we arrived at the ranch house, I saw Luke looking at me and he smiled and winked. I smiled in return. He and the other hands were cleaned up and dressed for the occasion, as was everyone else. It was lovely to see the festive decorations and everyone wearing their best. Julia, especially, sparkled in her holiday finery, a long wine-colored skirt with a lovely white lacy blouse. She was wrapped in a dark shawl that matched her skirt. Her auburn curls were tied back with a ribbon. I noticed the men smiling in her direction. Julia is so beautiful! Cora will need to watch out for her with a barnful of men nearby!

What a fun time we had! Patrick and Cora had put together quite a spread, augmented by the additions of specialty foods from Martha and Mary, Clay and Fletcher's wives. Several people had made small toys and dolls for the younger children.

To my great surprise, Fletcher brought out a fiddle after dinner and played some rousing jigs and a waltz or two. Although there wasn't much space, we pushed back the tables and chairs and the children happily danced around the room. It was quite hilarious.

Chapter Sixteen: January 1899

The coldest month came in January. The first light snows had begun in late November, but now they were steady and unrelenting. High winds piled the snow in drifts around our cabin, chicken coop, the ranch house and barn. James had to put on snowshoes to get down to the barn, and even then, it was a struggle. All the cattle were sheltered and the horses too. The men spent hours piling hay up for them.

A few nights it was so bad James just stayed at the barn and left me alone. My biggest worry was going into labor. How could James leave me alone this way? What kind of a man would do that to his wife? Cold and alone, I wished I had someone I could count on by my side. I kept the cowbell close by.

When the wind was fierce, I was so grateful for the bales of hay that sheltered the cabin and chickens. This was not like the winters I remembered in New Hampshire. It certainly snowed there but the temperatures here were brutal when the wind blew! At any given time, it seemed like three to four feet of snow and possibly more against the outside wall of our cabin and the chicken coop. It was exceedingly difficult to make a trip to the necessary. At least I could dump the chamber pot close by.

James, Luke, and some of the others went up and down the path they had made earlier to our cabin to keep it clear enough to traverse on skis or snowshoes. They also made smaller paths to the necessary and the chicken coop. James grudgingly stayed after the others went back to the barn. I no longer worried about what would happen when my time came.

As the month progressed, I was cozy in my snowed-in "cave". James checked on me, during the day, and I was content. I spent my time baking bread, making stew, and preparing everything I would need for the birth. By late-January, I was so unwieldy I could barely move. A storm was brewing. I could feel it in my bones, and I began to panic again. However, James had checked the path, and all seemed well.

On the twenty-first, after James had left in the morning, I felt a wave of pain come over me and water ran down my leg. I managed to get to the door and screamed for help into the wind. Then I remembered the bell and staggered over to where it was hanging on the wall. I lifted it off its nail and took it to the door where I rang it as loudly as I could. I had no way of knowing if anyone heard me. I screamed a few more times and rang the bell until I felt the need to lie down. I managed to get a kettle of water onto the stove, then crept to my bed. At least I had the presence of mind to grab the clean sheets that had been prepared for this moment and spread them across my bed as best I could.

I cried out in pain lying curled up on my bed,

panting, resting, then screaming again with every wave. Just when I thought all hope was lost, Cora arrived with Julia. James arrived a few moments later. The three of them came on snowshoes.

"Good thing you rang the bell when you did," James said. "The snow is starting to pick up. We may all be here a while." He came to stand by the bed and touched my shoulder. I was panting hard but was much relieved to have help.

Immediately, Cora took over. She made me her tea, much stronger this time, and I rested for a little while after drinking it until stronger pains came. Julia saw to the boiling water and handed a hot wet towel to Cora to wash her hands. Cora laid out her scissors and towels and sat at the foot of the bed, moving her skillful hands as needed.

I was surprised to find that James, at Cora's direction, had come to sit behind me on the bed, his legs to either side of my hips, his arms held tightly around my shoulders. Despite the pain, I felt safe in his arms and was filled with gratitude that he had chosen to be with me after all. I could hear Julia in the kitchen filling the stove with coal and boiling more water. Then she came beside me and held my legs.

Cora talked to me in a soft voice of encouragement. I heard her as if I were far away. Every so often I felt James wipe my face with a damp cloth. The pains still came in waves, and finally I was told to push. There was more pain, I panted and gasped for air, and was told to push again, harder. I felt like I was going to rip apart. I thought the pain would never stop, and I could hear myself screaming. James continued to hold me tightly. The pains went on until I did not think I could stand it anymore. Tears streamed down my face and James wiped them away.

At last, I felt the final rush and Cora exclaimed, "The baby is coming. I can see the head!" In a stream of blood and mucous, I could feel my baby rushing into the light. Cora said, "Congratulations! You have a beautiful baby girl!" She was grinning.

James relaxed his hold on me and prepared to get up. "Well done," he said gruffly, then, "I am glad that is over with!" He stood up and moved towards the door. Cora tied a string around the baby's cord and cut it, then swaddled her in a soft blanket. "Here she is," she said as she handed the tiny bundle to me. "She is a beauty, just like her mama! And look, she has her papa's dark hair. James, come look at your new daughter." He made no move to come closer. Julia approached me and the baby. She touched my hand and murmured, "Blessings upon you and your sweet little girl. You have done well."

I was exhausted and slipped into a hazy sleep. When I awoke, I found myself cradling my lovely baby girl against my chest. She was trying to nurse, and I opened my night dress to help her. She had trouble latching on and no milk appeared.

"Why is there no milk?" I asked Cora. "Is something wrong?"

"It usually takes some time for the milk to come. You are doing fine. Rest and let nature work its magic. Have you decided on a name yet?"

I looked at James. Remarkably, he was still standing by the door, looking like he was ready to flee. We had not discussed a name since he had shown so little interest in the subject. He looked blank in return.

"I like the name Emma. I would like to call her Emma Louise." I looked again at James and he nodded.

"Emma Louise Parker. It is a good name," I said. I was pleased to see the corners of James's mouth lift in a small smile.

Chapter Seventeen

James went down to the barn in the blinding snow soon after to give everyone the news. I heard later that there was celebrating among the hands that included a considerable amount of beer. James did not reappear that night, but Cora came to see how I was doing that evening. She brought a small gift, a soft little snuggly "nappy" cloth for the baby to hold against her face.

Cora was entranced by Emma. "I hope I have another wee babe one day. It is so lovely to hold an infant in your arms," she said softly.

I recovered quickly, for which I was grateful. I suppose that being young and strong helped, and I was greatly relieved when Emma figured out how to nurse and the milk came easily. Cora returned two days after my delivery to check on me and the baby. Julia was with her.

"You are to be congratulated," Cora said. "You are already up and about. I am proud of you!"

The three of us cooed over little Emma and she rewarded us with a loud burp. She looked at us solemnly through enormous hazel eyes–as if she were seeing us from far away. I could not get enough of that look.

Julia spoke to me, her eyes on the floor. "I was wondering", she said softly, "if you would like some help with the baby during the day when your husband is working. I would be happy to come for a few hours every day or two and help with cooking or laundry or feeding the chickens while you get back on your feet. Would you like that?"

I looked quickly at Cora to see if she had put Julia up to this, but she was smiling at Julia in support.

"That would be helpful, Julia. Thank you for offering, though I really have nothing I can give you in return. Perhaps for a couple of weeks till I am used to being a mother." I did not have the heart to tell her I had helped raise four of my younger siblings from birth until I left home. I suddenly realized how much I missed them. Julia was only a year older than my half-sister, Becky, and not much younger than me. Gratitude filled my heart.

That evening at dinner, while Emma was asleep in her basket in the other room, I told James about Julia's offer.

"That would be fine," he said gruffly. "If it will help you".

"I am grateful for her offer. I think I will enjoy her company."

After a few minutes of silence, I said, "James,

what made you change your mind about helping at the birth? I thought you were angry with me and did not want anything to do with the baby. I actually thought I was losing you." My throat caught as I said this.

"I had a long talk with Luke. He was annoyed with me for the way I have been treating you these past few months. I truly do not know what was going through my head, but I think I was jealous of the baby, somehow, taking all your attention and changing your body from the beautiful slender girl I fell in love with to an unwieldy and grotesque version of your former self." I flinched.

"In any case, I know it was wrong of me, so when I heard you scream for help and ring the bell, I determined I should be there. Please forgive me." He put his head down on the table and I could not help but take his hands in mine and say softly, "I forgive you."

He reached out his hand and touched my arm, then moved up to my neck. He caressed my cheek. "When," he asked, "how long?" He had a twinkle in his eyes.

"Give me a few weeks," I said, blushing. "I miss you too".

Chapter Eighteen

Life went on as before, with the added joy of a happy baby and the company of Julia several afternoons a week. James held me in his arms at night, although it was too soon yet for more than that. I was grateful he did not insist. My cup overflowed with happiness. Oh, how I had missed being close to James and I longed for us to return to the ways we had loved before Emma changed our lives. Still, he had no interest in the baby, did not want to hold her, did not even look into her face, or smile at her. He became annoyed when I tried to encourage him to spend a little time with her. That was the one thing that saddened me during that time.

As the days passed into March, I was heartened to see the days growing longer and the snow beginning to recede. I went outside on sunny days with Emma well wrapped in blankets to get a little exercise. I also wanted to check on the new holding tank, to see if the snow was melting in that direction. I was rewarded with a pool of shallow water, or sometimes ice, in the lower end of the basin. I was elated.

I came to look forward to the days Julia would be with me. She always had a smile on her face and sometimes sang to herself as she went about feeding the chickens scraps from the kitchen or washing all those soiled nappies - not even those could bring her down! Nothing I asked her to help me with or do on her own fazed her. She was wonderful with Emma and Emma always smiled and chortled with glee when Julia appeared at our cabin.

Julia was a breath of fresh air after feeling stifled by James. I greatly enjoyed our conversations. She asked me about growing up with my family in New Hampshire and told me what it was like on the ranch when she was little. I appreciated not having to be careful what I said when we were together like I did with James. I began to relax and simply enjoy my days with my baby and Julia when James was not at home.

The one thing I thought odd during this time was that James found many reasons why he needed to go into Flagstaff during the week. Usually, he took a wagon and said he needed to pick up supplies for Patrick or the men. I did not know much about these trips, and I chose not to ask questions. I also noticed that the jar in which we put James's monthly cash stipend was empty, more often than not. I did not want to know why.

Chapter Nineteen

One day in mid-April, when Emma was almost three months old and the weather was fine, I brought the baby down to the ranch house and then the barn to show her off. I could feel spring in the air, and I walked down the path with a light step. Emma was growing fast. She was wide eyed, taking everything in.

At the house, Cora and Patrick were delighted to see the baby.

"May I hold her?" Cora asked almost immediately and Patrick too. Emma was the first infant on the ranch in several years. I think they were almost as delighted as I was.

"Oh, I miss having an infant in my arms," cooed Cora. "Maybe we need another little one in our family." She winked at Patrick and he winked back.

I wish James could be this happy. He rarely holds Emma, and then only for a few minutes.

Cora presented me a lovely hand embroidered

blanket of soft natural wool with colorful flowers and vines twisting around the edges and filling the corners.

"Oh, this is so beautiful," I said. "But it is too much–I can't accept this–it must have taken you hours to make!"

"Nonsense! I love doing this kind of handwork and it helped me pass the time during the long winter months. Besides, your beautiful baby deserves something beautiful to wrap herself in." I was fighting tears and gave her a big hug of appreciation.

When I went down to the barn, everyone exclaimed over the baby.

"How beautiful she is, just like her mama."

"My, what a smile."

"Look at that dark hair and those big eyes."

"You and James have done well for yourselves." I drank in the compliments. It was a long time since anyone had said such words to me, even if it was all about Emma.

One of the hands, Clay, I think, said there was a new litter of puppies, and asked if we wanted to see them. My heart leaped. Of course, we did! In one of the stalls, the mama licked and caressed her pups while they squirmed and nursed and climbed over each other. I counted seven.

"Oh, my–quite a litter!" I was already in love. The puppies were mostly black and white, like my beloved

Sunny, the Border Collie I had grown up with. Who knew what these sweet puppies were, although the mother was certainly a herding dog. I just knew I had to have one. The puppy could keep me company when James was working and alert me to visitors. Emma was intrigued, stretching her little arm out to the puppies.

"How old are they," I asked.

"Only a week. Would you like one when they are ready?"

"Oh, yes! May I come and visit a few times before I choose?"

"Of course," Clay said.

I decided I wanted a female pup. She would have to be smart, like Sunny had been, and good with babies. I already had a name in mind.

That evening when James returned for supper, he was in a good mood. I smelled alcohol on his breath, which was becoming a frequent occurrence, and I was not pleased. However, since he seemed to be in good spirits, I told him about the puppies.

"Have you seen them, James? They are in one of the horse stalls, about one week old. They are SO cute! Mostly black with white markings. They remind me a little of Sunny when I was growing up. Do you remember me telling you about him?"

"No, I haven't seen them yet. I was out on the range most of these past few days."

"Please look at them when you get a chance, maybe tomorrow morning? I was thinking it would be nice to have a puppy at the house to keep me and Emma company. She could announce visitors and warn us of any strangers or wild animals coming near us. And…"

"Ok, Ok, I will think about it," James said gruffly, his mood suddenly changing to something darker. I said nothing more. I had learned when it was best for me to keep my mouth shut when his mood changed. I did not want to be the brunt of his annoyance. I felt sad that we had such different views on things. Besides, we had several weeks before they would be old enough to leave their mother. I resolved to be patient.

Chapter Twenty

One morning in May, James drove Emma and me into town. I wanted to show Emma off to Blue and to Grace. I had missed seeing them over the long winter. I had also sorely missed seeing the larger world around us, after being cooped up for so long. I was more than ready to "fly the nest"! In every direction the signs of spring brought new color to the land with wildflowers just starting to bloom. The mountain peaks still had their snow caps. It was a breathtaking scene all around us.

James dropped me off at Blue's shop while he went to pick up more feed for the chickens and other provisions for our family. I had been especially craving fresh vegetables but doubted there would be any available this early in the season.

Blue and Grace were entranced with Emma, who, despite the long drive was in a happy mood. She entertained us with gurgles and flailing arms.

"Oh, Sarah," Blue said. "She is so precious. And she has your eyes and James's dark hair." She paused.

"How does James feel about her now that she is here? I remember you saying the last time we met he was not interested in the coming baby at all."

"Something interesting happened shortly before she was born. I still cannot quite believe it! Apparently, James's friend Luke had a heart-to-heart talk with James and told him he had been treating me poorly. I do not know the details, but James seems to have taken what Luke said to heart. When my time came and I rang my bell for help, James came. He sat behind me and held me tight during my pains while Cora and Julia helped me do my part. I felt so safe and loved. It was wonderful. And thanks to the tea Cora gave me, the pains were not more than I could bear most of the time!"

"That is wonderful to hear, Sarah. we have been worried about you and James, to be truthful," said Grace.

"Thank you both. I have been as well. It is hard to say how we will fare in the future, but right now we are happy enough and for that I am grateful. One step in front of the other, my mother used to say."

Just then Blue clapped her hands. "I just remembered there is an itinerant photographer in town, just for a few days. You and James and the baby should get your portrait taken!"

"Oh, I would love that," said. "I will ask James when he comes for me."

When James arrived, I told him about the photographer and that he would only be in town for a few days.

"Let's take Emma and have a family portrait taken!" I was excited by the prospect and James agreed. We went up the main street several blocks until we saw the wagon that held the photographer's equipment.

The photographer was an elderly gentleman with wild white hair and a long beard. He quickly invited us into his makeshift studio.

"What a beautiful family you have!" he exclaimed gleefully. "How old is your little girl?"

"She is almost four months old," I said. "Her name is Emma Louise".

"How lovely," he said.

Meanwhile, James was impatient to get the photos taken so we could get on our way home.

"Just sit here Mrs -?"

"Parker" I said. I sat Emma on my lap. Her high-pitched giggle made us laugh.

"And Mr. Parker? Stand right here behind your lovely wife and little daughter".

While he was setting up his camera, I asked the gentleman where he came from. "Do you have a home base or just travel from place to place?

"I come from everywhere and nowhere," he replied. "There is no particular place I belong."

"Really?" I asked.

"I just keep moving. I may go down to Phoenix, which I hear is growing into a big town, or I may go west to California. Then again, I might go east to Albuquerque. Someday I may find where I belong, and when I do, I will know I am home."

We paid the man his fee, and he said we could pick up our prints in a few days.

"What a peculiar man," James remarked, sullenly, when we were headed home.

"I thought he was quite interesting," I responded. "I can't wait to see our portrait." I liked the old man's philosophy—that he will know when he is home when he gets there.

Chapter Twenty-One

A few days later, I persuaded Patrick to let me drive the wagon to Flagstaff alone to pick up our photographic portrait and visit Blue. I promised James I would only visit with Blue briefly and would pick up the portrait prints from the itinerant photographer as quickly as possible. I would take Emma with me. He was not happy about this prospect but eventually agreed, since he had so much to do with the cattle on the range. At his insistence, I took the rifle with me. When we left, he said he would be watching for our return. It was my first time away from the ranch by myself, and I found it exhilarating. I am completely on my own for these few hours! Just Emma and me. This thought caught me by surprise.

I was so excited to see our portrait and was well rewarded with a wonderful photograph when I picked up the prints. There we were, James and me and our beautiful baby Emma in crisp black and white mounted on a decorated cardboard backing. As requested, there were two copies. How amazing to see our little family rendered in such style!

I showed the portraits to Blue and Grace. They loved them too.

"You and Emma look so happy," Blue said. "And James looks quite handsome, though not as happy as you. What a lovely memento you have."

"Thank you again for telling me about the itinerant photographer! I love this photograph of my little family. And I was pleased Emma behaved so well. By the way, the photographer told me an unusual thing when we first met him. He just travels from place to place. No family, no home. He said to me, 'someday I may find where I belong, and when I do, I will know I am home.' Can you imagine? I could never be comfortable living like that!"

"Nor I," said Grace. "I love my home here and my life—our life together!" she said, looking at Blue with affection. "I can't imagine being completely untethered like that."

"This story reminds me a little of my own story and why I left home.

"My father was killed in a terrible accident when I was about two and my brother Jacob was four. Our lives changed completely after that. My mother was devastated, though of course, at my age, I could not have understood that. She became very distant and had no time for us. Eventually, a few years later, she married a man named Ben, who became my stepfather. He and my mother had four children soon after they married, and my mother became increasingly busy as her quilt pattern business grew. Although I loved my half siblings and helped take care of them, I no longer knew how I fitted into the family. As I got older, I became angry and felt I needed to find a place of my own where I belonged.

"I was sixteen when I met James. I got carried away by his charm and his promises and thought he could be the answer to my dilemma. His dream of becoming a wrangler on a western ranch became my dream. And here I am for better or worse."

"Thank you for sharing that with me," Blue said, giving me a hug. "I had a feeling something like that might have happened. I hope you will be able gain some clarity about what you want and need in your life."

I returned her hug. "Thank you, Blue. You have no idea how much your support, and Grace's means to me. I would love to hear your story sometime, too."

"We would be happy to share it. Have a safe trip home."

Before returning to the ranch, I determined that I would write home to Mama and my family and let them all know about our lives here in Arizona Territory.

June 18*th*, 1899

Dearest Mama,

I miss you and the family most sorely. I also want you to know we are well and that our lives here in the Arizona Territory suit us nicely.

James and I were married in Flagstaff as soon as we arrived. We found a wonderful position on a ranch not far from town. James is a ranch hand and I take care of a large flock of chickens and a vegetable garden to feed us all. Most important of everything else, we have a lovely daughter, born January 21. Her name is Emma Louise. We had this wonderful portrait taken when Emma was about five months old. We are so happy and have a good life. We have a small but comfortable cabin to live in and many friends.

What a lovely coincidence that today is my 19*th* birthday! I am feeling very grown up! My friend Blue has gifted me with a lovely scarf. It was she who told me about the photographer.

We hope you are all well and that you will think fondly of us. I love you all and hope to hear from you when you can.
You can send mail to us at Mr. and Mrs. James Parker, care of P. McBride, Post office, Flagstaff, Arizona Territory.

All my love.
Your daughter, Sarah

I purchased an envelope and stamp at the post office and mailed my letter with a copy of our portrait enclosed. It had been a year since I last saw Mamma and my family. It felt good to reopen communication with them, and it was my birthday! My heart sang.

When I returned home, I drew forth the birthday gift that I had tucked away in my bag for myself. A small locket that opened. I loved it. One day it would hold a photo of Emma. At dinner, I discovered that James had not remembered. I was disappointed but not surprised. I decided to say nothing.

I had been taking Emma down to the barn every week since the puppies were born, to see how they were growing and developing. After just a few weeks I could see their personalities beginning to show – which ones were outgoing, most playful, aggressive, or shy. Four of the puppies were female, so I paid most of my attention to them. We would stand outside the wood gate to the stall and watch the puppies through the slats.

One of the hands had thrown a few toys into the stall and it was fun to see the puppies tussling with each other over who could play with them. All the while their mother, Sammy, short for Samantha, kept careful watch over the puppies and me while I talked to her and petted one or another of the funny little creatures through the slats. The smallest of the females seemed to spend most of her time either with her mother or along the walls of the stall. I watched her closely to see if she would lose some of her shyness as she got older.

One afternoon, Julia and I went together to see them. While Julia held Emma, I went into the stall, carefully, so as not to frighten Sammy, and leaned down to let the puppies smell me. Luke and Clay stopped by to watch.

"Have you picked out your favorite yet?" Luke asked. I gently lifted the smallest one and cradled her in my arms. She did not seem at all nervous, which was a good sign.

"I am thinking about this little girl," I said. "She is a bit shy, but I don't want a dog that is too rambunctious or aggressive around the baby. She and Emma can grow up together. I will ask James when he gets home tonight."

Luke looked at me for a moment, his back turned to Julia and Clay. "I hope James will approve," he said softly and raised one eyebrow in question. I smiled and nodded to him.

"I am sure everything will be fine" I said.

He nodded in turn with a small smile. "Just let me know if you have any problems. With the puppy".

"I will, Luke. Thank you for looking out for us." A warm feeling spread through me, and I said a silent prayer of gratitude for Luke's friendship. I wish James could be more like Luke–kind and thoughtful. This thought caught me off guard.

To my surprise, James said yes to adopting the puppy.

"She looks OK," he said. "I think she will make a good companion for you and Emma. Just don't ask me to clean up after her when she makes a mess in the house."

"I promise I won't. Oh, thank you James." I clapped my hands and did a little dance in happiness.

Chapter Twenty-Two

Julia sometimes came to us on horseback, even though it was only a short walk up from the house. Her horse was a beautiful young mare, with brown and white markings. She was gentle and friendly and made me homesick for Molly, my mother's mare with whom I had grown up. I wondered now if it would be painful since I had given birth only six months before.

I spoke of this with Julia one afternoon while we were busy washing nappies and bedding in a large pot of boiling water over the fire pit and hanging them up to dry in the sun.

"Julia—when I was a child, I lived on a farm for a while before my family moved into town. We had a wonderful mare named Molly that my mother had raised from a filly when she was about your age. I used to ride her when I got big enough. I would like to try riding again. What do you think?"

"I think it would be wonderful," Julia said with enthusiasm. "You could start with riding my horse, Autumn, and see how you feel. Perhaps there is a horse down at the barn that you could borrow."

I put on the split skirt that Blue had made for me and came to stand beside Julia's beautiful mare. I put my foot tentatively into the stirrup on the left side and lifted myself gingerly into the saddle, something I had not done since I was a child. It felt so right. I was elated. We took a few steps together and then stopped. What if James came home early? He won't be happy about this.

I began riding Autumn short distances when Julia brought her to the cabin. There was still snow on the ground, so we walked carefully. It had been years since I had ridden a horse, and the saddle style was not familiar to me. However, I soon adjusted, and the saddle felt comfortable, like being with an old friend. Of course, I was a little sore at first, but gradually my body adjusted to this new way of holding myself. I longed to go faster and farther but determined to be patient until I had spoken to James and I made sure Julia took Autumn down to the barn before I expected James to come home.

I decided I must speak to James about borrowing a horse from the barn to ride. I brought up the subject at dinner one night when he seemed in a good mood.

"James, do you remember me telling you how I used to ride my mother's horse, Molly, when I was a child? And that time when we were courting that you let me ride with you on your horse, Midnight? Julia has a lovely mare that I have been riding, recently, just a little, around our cabin. It reminded me of how much I enjoyed riding when I was younger."

"How can you ride? You just had a baby?"

"Well, I considered that and have been careful. It has been almost six months and I am feeling fine. Oh, James, I have been loving being on horseback again. Maybe you could come riding with me? Or, if I could borrow a horse from the barn, Julia could ride with me. It would be so much fun."

"If Julia went with you who would watch the baby?"

"Maybe Cora would. She loves Emma! What do you say?"

"I don't know what to say. I will have to think about it."

"Think about this, then." I said, annoyed." Your wife loves to ride and is good at it. She needs something to do besides staying home with an infant and feeding chickens while her husband gets to ride the range chasing cattle all day."

James scowled. "Just don't complain to me if you get injured when you get thrown or lost.!"

"I promise!"

Chapter Twenty-Three

Julia helped me prepare and plant the garden once again. She showed me how to carry Emma on my back Indian style. She had learned how to make a so-called papoose from a picture book about Indian life she had found in the library in Flagstaff. Together we made a papoose that held the baby snugly against my back but facing out, leaving her arms and legs free and giving her more to look at as we moved around. She seemed to enjoy this mode of travel, but I could feel her growing weight on my back.

We planted a variety of root vegetables and I decided to experiment with winter and summer squash. I was not yet familiar with this soil or the climate, but at least water was not an issue yet, thanks to the annual summer monsoons. We also planted many sunflower seeds. They had done well the previous summer, and the chickens loved the seed heads in the fall. Again, we tried spinach, chard, and several types of lettuce, providing them with a bit of shade made by a trellis I built over them on which I planted cucumbers.

Julia convinced me to plant some Indian corn for the chickens as well. Her mother gave me some seeds.

I wondered if the sweet corn I grew up with in New Hampshire would grow here. Perhaps I can get some seeds from my family. After consulting with Cora, I decided to try several varieties of tomatoes, as well, and see which ones grew best. The tomato sauces she made were amazing if a bit hot for my eastern taste. I did not plant any chili peppers! Sweet peppers were enough for me!

After spending a good part of every day in the garden, Julia and I would go riding together for an hour or two. I had persuaded Luke and Clay to let me ride one of the smaller and gentler horses, a grey named Shadow. With Emma strapped into my lap, face forward, it was like heaven when Julia and I took off across the prairie, the wind in our hair, no one to tell us what to do. I think that was the happiest I had been in a long time. I would return home exhilarated, face flushed, hair a mess, Emma giggling. James scowled but said nothing.

Chapter Twenty-Four

When the puppies were eight weeks old, Julia and Emma and I went to bring our new family member home. I had decided some time ago to call her "Luna", after the moon, and in honor of my very first puppy friend "Sunny" when I was a child. I hoped that Luna could be such a friend for Emma and our family.

When I scooped Luna up into my arms, I told Sammy she could visit anytime and that I would bring Luna to see her too. Somehow, I think she understood me. I had made Luna a collar, which I placed around her neck with a lead attached, and we walked home along the path to the cabin surrounded by long grass. Emma babbled excitedly and Luna sniffed everything. We made quite the procession.

I remembered some of how my mother trained Sunny and we began the very next day training Luna. The puppy was very quick to pick up what I wanted her to do and, more importantly, not do. I made her a bed in the kitchen, which she immediately abandoned to sleep in our bedroom. I also made her a long lead that I attached to the kitchen door so she could venture some distance from the cabin but not too far. We made a great team. I was surprised to find I loved her almost as much as I loved my own baby girl. My heart is full!

Every morning after I nursed Emma and made breakfast, I took Luna for a walk on her lead around our little "homestead". Emma accompanied us on my back in the "papoose". When I worked in the garden, I allowed Luna to run free and quickly taught her not to run into the garden.

"Go around"! I instructed her and after a few scolds and directions, she understood! She would run around the perimeter of the garden to the point nearest where I was and sit there and I would then give her a small treat and lots of praise. She also learned the basic commands of Come and Stay right away. It was amazing. What a smart girl!

Luna and Emma soon became great friends. Luna slept next to her at night and watched her closely during the day. When I was nursing Luna was right there, attentive. If Emma awoke in her basket and cried, Luna went back and forth between the baby and me until I came and picked Emma up to feed her or change her nappies. Emma often laughed and cooed happily while Luna cuddled up close to her. Their relationship was so much like mine as a child with Sunny. What a joy to watch them together.

Chapter Twenty-Five

One morning, after I had tended to Emma and the chickens, I heard the beat of horses' hooves down by the barn. I looked out and saw three men who were speaking with someone by the barn door and then they headed up the path towards our cabin. I quickly removed my soiled apron and attempted to fix my hair, which was in a long braid over my left shoulder.

As the men came closer, I was astonished to recognize my brother Jacob! I cried out in happiness and ran towards the men.

"Oh Jacob," I cried. "What are you doing here?" I gave him a big hug and we whirled around together for a minute.

"We wanted to surprise you! These are my friends Nat and Tom, James's brothers!" And to them "This is my long-lost sister Sarah!" The young men jumped down from their horses and each took one of my hands and kissed it. I blushed.

Luna, meanwhile, was going crazy with happiness

to meet these new friends, jumping up and giving her little welcome bark.

"Oh my, welcome, welcome" I said. "And this is Luna–as you can see, she bids you welcome also." I gestured towards our cabin.

"It isn't much, but it is ours," I said, blushing, as they entered our kitchen. "James is out on the range today, but I expect him back for dinner. I hope you can wait to visit with him. He will be thrilled to see you, I am sure!" I chattered on, made nervous by this unexpected visit.

Both brothers were tall and lean like James and had similar dark wavy hair. Nat had a mustache as well. They wore traveling clothes that looked like they had been slept in for the entire trip, which was likely the case. Jacob, too, was wearing a suit I did not recognize and looked worn out after their long trip. They apparently came directly from the train station, after getting directions and hiring horses. They carried little baggage, so it appeared they would not be staying long.

"Perhaps Nat and Tom could wait for James down by the barn and we could spend some time together," Jacob said to me.

"That sounds wonderful," I said. "But first, wait right here. You have not yet met your little niece, Emma!"

Emma was just waking from her nap and I picked her up to show her off. She looked sleepy but brightened when she saw the new faces.

"This is Emma Louise," I said with great pride. "She is almost seven months now and is crawling everywhere. She is a delight."

Jacob took Emma in his arms and lifted her up with a whoop. Emma giggled.

"What a beautiful child," Jacob said. "She looks just like her beautiful mama!"

Then Nat and Tom asked for their turn holding Emma and whirling her around in the air. Emma chortled and laughed for each in turn.

"It looks like you and James have a lovely family here," said Nat. "Congratulations to you and our brother."

I invited the three of them to join me for lunch and we had an enjoyable meal while I began to get to know James's brothers. But I could not take my eyes off Jacob. It just seemed so unreal that he was here in my own little cabin, Then I asked the brothers to wait down by the barn for James to come back after his day on the range.

"There are likely some of the hands working nearby that you can talk to, if you like," I said. "Feel free to look around." They agreed, taking the horses down with them.

After they had left, I spread a blanket on the tall grass outside the door of our cabin and Jacob sat down with me, Emma in his lap. Luna settled down next to us, keeping her eyes on Emma. The day was warm and the view towards the barn and the mountains beyond was lovely.

"I can certainly see why you love this place." Jacob said when we were settled. "It is beautiful here–so different from home, which, I suppose, was one of the things you were after." He smiled, but then got serious. "So, is your dream of being here in the Arizona Territory with James what you had hoped for?"

"Well Jacob, my answer is not easy. Yes, I love my new life here. I love my position here, my new friends and my little girl. Life with James, on the other hand, has been both wonderful and not so good. I am not sure what to tell you."

"In what way not so good," Jacob asked me. He laid a hand on my arm.

"I love James, and I think he loves me, but he shows little interest in Emma, which I find hard to understand. How could he not adore this precious child? He does not pick her up or even smile to her. He loves being a wrangler and has made good friends among the hands. However, he drinks a great deal and can't seem to leave alcohol alone. He is moody and finds fault with me often over little things. He can get angry when he has been drinking. Sometimes he is so loving and other times I hardly know him and that scares me."

Jacob put his arms around me. "I am so sorry to hear this, Sarah. It is good you have friends here to talk to."

"Oh, Jacob," I said. "I have missed you and all of our family. I only regret how much I hurt everyone by what I did. I know it was wrong. I was just so desperate to get away, and it felt so right at the time. I have grown up this past year. I am no longer the child who was taken care of by others."

"I can certainly see how much effort you have put into building your home and your life here. You have matured so much since I last saw you. You were just an impetuous young girl and now you are a wife and mother. It is hard to fathom."

"Yes. Now I am responsible for my family, my husband, and my baby! As for James, I think he was happy to get away from home, and I know he likes ranching and enjoys his friendships among the hands. There is just something I can't quite put my finger on. He angers so easily. Like I said, there are times when I feel like he is a stranger. Did Nat or Tom talk about James at all?"

"Not much, though they did say he was pretty anxious to leave home. Apparently, he was not happy there. I think they were hoping that making a new life with you would turn things around for him. Has James ever talked to you about what it was like for him at home before he brought you here?" When I shook my head, he said, "see if you can get him to open up a little. Maybe there is something there that he is keeping hidden."

"I tried when we were on the train coming west. He got annoyed at my questions. He is a hard man to talk to, sometimes. He does not like to talk about himself."

While carrying Emma, I gave Jacob a tour of our

small homestead, the house, the chicken coup, and my big garden. Luna raced happily back and forth as we walked.

"Do you know I was a bit panicked when we first arrived?" I said, laughing at the memory. "Overnight I had to take care of everything–I–who had never even cooked a meal in my life! Thank goodness Cora was willing to teach me how to cook!" I grinned, pleased with myself at all I had accomplished in the past year.

Jacob hugged me. "You have done well, little sister."

"So now, you must catch me up on everything that is happening at home."

After a dinner of scrambled eggs cooked with fresh vegetables and cheese, I made a bedroll in our kitchen for Jacob. It was nice knowing he would be sleeping nearby, and we talked late into the night. I was happy to hear about Alice, the young woman Jacob had fallen in love with and their plans to build up and expand our father's farm. Soon they would be married.

Nat and Tom ate dinner with James and the men at the ranch house and spent the night at the barn with James, and that felt right. James told me later he was surprised and happy to see his brothers again, and they had a grand reunion that naturally involved a few beers.

The next day Patrick offered all three of them positions as ranch hands, but Jacob declined, citing his upcoming marriage.

"I am working the farm my father built, but I am much obliged. This is a beautiful place and I know my sister is happy here." Both Tom and Nat happily accepted Patrick's offer of employment

"This is a wonderful opportunity for us," said Nat. "And it will be nice working with our brother James again, not to mention spending time with his beautiful wife and baby daughter."

Jacob stayed for several days and it was like heaven having him close by. It seemed we never ran out of things to talk about. At night James chose to sleep in the barn with his brothers. I did not mind. But for some reason Jacob's continued presence annoyed him. Is he jealous, or does not want Jacob snooping into his life?

"Does Becky still love to take photographs? Please ask her to take lots of our siblings and especially of mama! Ben, too," I added. "Send news. I will stay in touch and let you know what is happening here, as well."

When Jacob was ready to leave, I gave him a letter to our mother and begged him to send photos of the family. Jacob promised. "Mama, especially, misses you more than you can imagine." We shared a long hug before he mounted his horse and rode away. I tried to keep a brave face but dissolved in tears as he left.

July 1899

Dearest Mother,

I have just had the most wonderful visit with Jacob! What a wonderful surprise to see him here! I will let him tell you all about my life on the ranch, but I do wish you could see your beautiful little granddaughter, Emma. She is the light of my life and my reason for being! She is just beginning to crawl now and talks non-stop in a mix of nonsense sounds She often giggles and laughs. She is a constant delight!

I absolutely love this ranch and my life here. It is beyond beautiful and I have made many friends. My only sorrow is that James loves his ranching life but does not seem to relish the life of a father and husband. He spends little time with Emma and me. I fear he is slipping away. I shared much with Jacob and will let him tell you the rest.

I miss you more than I can ever say, and I am seriously considering coming East to visit all of you, when I have a better understanding of where my marriage stands.
Wish me well. I love you.

Your daughter, Sarah

Chapter Twenty-Six: September 1899

Julia helped me harvest our small bounty in September. I had planted a lot of root vegetables, carrots, beets, and turnips, which we stored in the cleaned-out root cellar. The sunflowers, of all different colors, were not quite ready to pick yet. I had not tried green beans or peas this season. Perhaps next year. The winter squash had grown well but needed more time to mature. The summer squash and greens we had planted did well. Thank goodness the summer monsoon rains had not failed, so watering had been easy.

The heat during the day was unrelenting, and I was beginning to feel tired, though I had not spoken of it yet. I was grateful the night brought relief. I laughed at the thought of complaining about being overcome by the heat when I remembered the icy cold and snow of the winter. I resolved to enjoy some part of every season. How different from my old home! I love it here, but I do miss the coolness of the woods, the soft humid air, and our little cabin by the lake. I miss swimming in the lake!

"Julia," I called to her across the garden. "I think it is time we had an adventure!"

"What do you mean?"

"Do you know how to swim?" I asked her.

"Yes," she said, her face lighting up.

"There is a place along the stream about a half mile from here where there is an opening in the Cottonwood trees. I think we could hide among the trees and swim without attracting attention. Do you want to try it?"

"Yes, of course! I will bring a blanket and towels. Oh, what fun!"

With Emma on my back and Luna running happily ahead, Julia and I soon came to the place James had not allowed me to swim when he went there with his friends. There was a small grassy clearing next to the water. The water was low and there was mud along the edge, but that did not stop us. I laid Emma on the blanket, and first Luna, then Julia and I jumped in the water with all our clothes on. What heaven!

The water was warm but refreshing. Keeping a watchful eye on the baby, I attempted to wash the dust out of my skirt and blouse. I was tempted to get my hair wet as well, but the color of the water did not appeal to me. My once white blouse was now streaky red/brown and clung to me. Julia was splashing and giggling, covered with mud, and Luna was frantic with joy and likewise dripping with mud.

I was moving back to the shore when I heard

horses. James appeared from between the trees, then Luke.

"What is the meaning of this," James said. "We have been watching you. You left the baby unattended while you made fools of yourself in the stream." I looked at James angry face and stiffened my back. Luke was behind James, and the look on his face was a contrast to James's. His eyes were full of mirth and it looked like he was trying not to laugh.

"James, are you serious? Do I really need to explain to you that after working in the garden all morning in this heat that we needed some refreshment and fun? Emma has never been out of my sight. Or Luna's, for that matter."

Julia looked downcast as she came out of the water, with Luna, dripping wet, following her. Luna helpfully shook herself and spread brown water droplets everywhere. At that, Luke could not help himself – he burst out laughing.

James grew red in the face. "Get yourselves cleaned up and get back to the house. Now." He wheeled his horse and left the clearing. I looked at Luke as if to say, "What the heck was that?"

Luke dismounted and said "Never mind. He's having a bad day". To Julia he said "It is OK– you won't be in any trouble for this. I will vouch for you. In fact, I am going to ask your father if you two can swim here whenever you want. Too bad we did not think of this earlier in the summer."

"Oh, Luke," I said. "Thank you. I have not had

this much fun in a long time!"

"You certainly do look a sight, soaking wet like that." He laughed and gave me an appraising look. "I wish I had one of those cameras I've heard about. I would show you off to everyone on this place."

I blushed crimson. "Thank goodness you don't! I am not looking forward to going home."

"I will see you later." He tipped his hat to me with a wink and nodded at Julia, then gave Luna an affectionate pat. "Now Luna needs a real bath along with you two." He walked his horse out of the clearing, then mounted and headed in the direction of our cabin.

I looked at Julia with a grin and we both burst into giggles. "Oh well, it was worth it, whatever James says. I guess we better head back, though, and see if we can get some of this mud out of our clothes and hair. Not to mention the mess Luna has made of herself." We gathered up Emma and the blanket and towels and headed back.

When we got to the garden and the water trough, we took buckets and splashed clean water over ourselves and the puppy, letting the muddy water drain into the garden. It took many buckets full to get a semblance of clean. We would have to do a real laundry when we got back to the house and wash our hair. We each filled pails with clean water to carry.

"What will your mother think when she sees your wet clothes and hair?"

"Oh, she knows me well—just another adventure,

I guess. Anyhow, that is what I hope she will think."
She laughed.

I could see two horses tied outside our cabin.
Thank goodness Luke is still there, I thought. I poured
my bucket of water into the large pot that hung over
the fire pit, and Julia did the same. I lit the kindling
under the wood and got a small fire going to heat the
water.

"Come", I said to Julia. "I will get something dry
for each of us to wear so we do not make a scandal
while we wash our clothes and underthings."

James met us at the door. He appeared to be in a
better mood, for which I was grateful.

"Sorry, Sarah. I guess you ladies deserve a little
fun once-in-a-while. I was just worried about the baby."

"I would never do anything to endanger Emma.
You must know that. And yes–we had a lot of fun.
More fun than I have had in many months." Why does
James always have to find fault with what I do? I am an
excellent mother, and he is hardly any kind of father!

"I was just leaving," Luke said, as he came out the
door.

"Good thing," Julia said. "We are just about to
strip off these wet clothes and get them into the hot
and soapy water."

"Oh", Luke said with a big grin. "Maybe I should
stay after all!"

Oh, my goodness. I blushed and could not help giggling.

"Shoo!" Julia and I said in unison, laughing.

Chapter Twenty-Seven

A few days later, I asked Julia to come with me and Emma to check out some berry bushes I had spotted the day we had our swimming adventure. I wondered if they were blackberries and if they were ripe yet. We were too far away to tell when I first saw them.

Carrying a basket and my rifle (I had determined to practice being safe), we headed along the stream, past our swimming place, until we reached a thicket of bushes near the water. Behind us were trees. I could see an abundance of berries, which did indeed look like blackberries, just coming ripe. It was tough to reach some of them because of the thorns, but we were able to quickly fill the basket. What a treasure!

We were chatting gaily, as we picked, and were just turning to head back the way we had come when Julia suddenly held a finger across her mouth. She scooped up Emma, who had been happily crawling around the little clearing we had made.

"Sarah," she hissed softly, "get your gun ready." I looked a question towards her.

"Bear," she mouthed. And sure enough, we soon heard the whuffing noise of a bear nearby.

As softly as I could, I cocked the rifle and made ready. I wondered if there were cubs nearby–if not, we might be OK. If we were between a mama bear and her cubs, we would be in serious trouble. Somehow, Julia kept Emma quiet, and I crouched, frozen, with the gun in my hands. Suddenly, I saw movement through the dense bushes and then heard a sort of mewling sound, something like a kitten. Instinctively, I raised the gun in the direction of the movement. Before I could pull the trigger, the bear charged and without thinking I fired once and then again. I heard her go down but still could not see her clearly. Then I heard the cub again, crying. I was shaking like a leaf.

Julia came beside me and put her arm around my shoulders. Emma started to cry. Julia handed her to me to soothe.

"You have done well," she told me. "I will check to make sure the sow is dead and find the cub." I reloaded the gun and handed it to her. I was shaking so hard I was having a hard time holding the bullets straight.

Julia returned shortly. "She is dead." I heaved a big sigh of relief.

"What about the cub?"

"I am afraid we will need to kill it too. It will not be able to survive without its mother. And I certainly do not wish to raise a baby bear!"

"I suppose so, though I do not stomach killing a baby."

"I will take care of it. It will not be the first time for me." Julia pushed through the bushes. I heard the shot and flinched.

As we gathered ourselves to return home, we heard horses coming near, then a "halloo" from beyond the trees. It sounded like Luke. There were other voices as well. Thank God someone has come!

Julia called out to him and we moved in his direction. Soon we could see Luke and Clay and Patrick. When they saw us, they dismounted and came running.

"What on earth has happened?" Patrick said, his voice almost frantic. "Julia are you all right?" His arms were around her in a tight hug.

Then Luke was holding my shoulders. He was trembling. "Are you alright?" he asked in a husky voice.

"Bear," I said, shaking. "And baby bear. I got the momma, just as she charged, and Julia got the baby. I think I may be sick" I leaned over and vomited.

Patrick went into the woods to where we had been and found the mother and cub, as we had said. He returned carrying the basket full of blackberries. With a twinkle in his eye, he asked, "Did you forget something?"

That evening, when James returned home, I

was feeling calmer, but could not get the image of the charging bear out of my mind. James said he had heard the story of the bear killing from Luke. It was all the talk among the men.

"I am glad you are alright, you and Julia," he said. "Good thing you are a crack shot with a rifle." He laughed and said nothing more. I went to bed early, after taking care of Emma and I pretended to be asleep when James joined me later. I could have been killed and that is all he can say? I stewed on that fact until I finally fell asleep.

A few days later everyone on the ranch was invited to a celebration, featuring bear steaks, bear meat stew, and blackberries. The skins were already cleaned and stretched outside. Julia and I were celebrated as heroes. I was totally embarrassed, but I think Julia enjoyed the attention. Luke, after a couple of beers, rose to give a toast.

"To Sarah and Julia, our intrepid bear hunters, for providing this feast. Who knew they were such great shots!" Then he did a funny pantomime of me fighting off a giant bear with my bare hands, then killing it with a single shot. I blushed. I saw James scowl.

Chapter Twenty-Eight

Later that week, sometime after I had fed Emma and put her down for the night, a loud noise came up from the barn and brought me running to the door of the cabin. There was shouting and sounds of banging and breakage. A fight? I grabbed my shawl and the baby, shutting Luna in the house, and ran down the hill to see what was happening. Clay saw me coming and ran towards me.

"Stay back, Sarah, you don't want to see this, and I don't want anything happening to you or the baby!"

"What is it, Clay? Is there anything I can do to help?"

"No, no. Take the baby home. You are better off there. One of us will come tell you about it soon." I heard loud cursing–James's voice, then Luke's and another crash. Then someone was yelling from the ranch house. Patrick McBride was running towards the barn. More cursing. It was all I could do not to run right into the barn, but Clay was right–I did not want any harm to come to Emma.

Back at the house, I put Emma in her basket and began pacing back and forth in our small kitchen. Then I went outside and paced in wide circles, keeping an eye on the barn door. My thoughts about what might be happening were eating me alive! James, drunk? Fighting?

Finally, all was quiet. I held my breath. No sounds. It was near midnight. I had already put Emma to bed, and she was sleeping soundly. I decided to get ready for bed myself.

Sometime after midnight, I heard soft voices outside. I got up to open the door, throwing my shawl over my nightdress. There was James, apparently unconscious, with Clay and Luke on either side, holding him up.

"Oh my god!" My hands flew to my mouth. "What is this?" I said in a loud whisper. "Here, bring him inside and put him on the bed and don't wake the baby!" Luke and Clay laid James down as gently as they could. He groaned but did not come to.

Back in the kitchen where there was some light, I looked at Luke, who was limping badly. He had bruises on his face, a black eye, and his nose was bleeding.

"Luke, you are a mess too! Let me clean you up a little." Luke sank into one of the chairs and I took a damp cloth and gently washed the worst of the blood off his face. "Here, hold this over your nose until it stops bleeding," I said, handing him a clean cloth. I was shaking.

"I need to tend to James now," I said. "Go on back

to the barn. We can talk about this tomorrow."

The next morning James was still sleeping when I awoke, but he appeared to be conscious. I crept quietly into the kitchen to start the coffee, then picked up Emma from her basket. She would be wailing soon, so I sat on the steps with her and began to nurse, to keep her mouth occupied. A little while later I laid her down while I got myself a cup of coffee, then held her in my lap again. She seemed content enough.

My mind was a whirl. What happened last night? What is going to happen when James wakes up? Should I confront him or just keep my mouth shut? I held tightly to Emma and rocked my body back and forth, trying to clear my head.

At last, I heard sounds coming from the kitchen and James appeared in the doorway with a cup of coffee. His face was badly swollen, and he looked sheepish.

"So," I said. "What happened last night?"

"I don't remember anything. Was it bad?" he asked.

"Yes," I said. "Very bad."

"What happened?"

"You apparently tried to get yourself killed is all, or tried to kill someone else," I retorted. "You are lucky you still have friends who were willing to save your neck and bring you home. You do not deserve them."

"Are you mad at me," James said plaintively.

"I don't even know what to say to you, James! Now go down to the barn and try to fix whatever it was you did. Don't come near us again until dinner!"

About noon, Luke appeared at my door. He was still limping, but his face was a little less swollen. I had just put Emma down for a nap and had started making bread.

Luke removed his hat. "I just came to make sure you and Emma are OK." He looked apologetic.

"We are fine." I said, shortly. "Tell me about last night. What the deuce happened?" My voice was unsteady.

"We had been just fooling around, having a few beers to celebrate the end of the week. Me and Clay and James and a couple of the other guys. We had been laughing, telling stupid jokes. Out of the blue, the tone changed. James had been drinking hard and seemed annoyed about something. Then he made a remark to me that made me angry. It just turned nasty real fast. It is hard to say what exactly happened until it was too late, and the fight was out of control." Luke hung his head and looked miserable. "I don't know what to say, Sarah. I am so sorry."

I considered this and then said, "what did James say to you that made you angry enough to start a big fight?"

"I don't want to say. I am just so sorry."

"Luke, I have to know," I said.

He hesitated. In a soft voice, he finally said, "James said I was paying too much attention to you and accused me of being in love with you. I think he just got crazy jealous. He looked angry enough to kill." Luke hid his face in his hands.

Finally, I had to ask, "Is what he said true?"

In a whisper, Luke said, "I see how he treats you. I can't stand it. You deserve so much better than that."

"Luke." I put my hand on his arm. "You know I care about you. You are a true friend. I don't know any more than that right now. Do you understand?"

"Yes." He got up to go. "I just wanted to let you know what happened last night."

"Thank you, Luke. I so appreciate the ways you have looked out for me and Emma. I wish..." Oh, how I wished I had met someone like Luke before I married James! How different my life would be, now.

He left, thankfully, before James returned to our cabin.

A few hours later, Cora and Patrick came to call on me, something they had not done since we first moved in.

"Do you have a few minutes to visit with us?" Cora asked.

"Of course. I will heat water for tea," I said to cover my nervousness. I invited them into my small kitchen, and they sat uncomfortably at the table.

"We heard the loud fight last night, and I went to investigate," Patrick began.

"First, is James alright? Are YOU alright?" Cora said.

"James is a mess, but I am OK. Thanks for your concern. I have spoken with Luke and he tried to explain what happened. I still do not fully understand. I know James can get out of control when he has drunk too much. I will speak to him tonight." My voice caught and tears stung my eyes.

"Cora and I want to assure you that whatever happens, you have a place here if you want it," Patrick said, and Cora nodded agreement. "However, you must know that this can't go on. Unless James can get control of himself, his days here are numbered."

"I understand. If I were in your shoes, I would say the same." Tears began to slide down my cheeks. "I am so sorry about this, and I am truly grateful for your support. I just wish I knew what to do." I began to sob.

Cora took my hand and said, "We will be glad to help, if we can."

When James returned for dinner, he was subdued

and contrite. His face still looked swollen and badly bruised, but not as bad as the night before. His knuckles were still bloody. I could not find it in my heart to be sympathetic.

"So, are you going to tell me what that was all about?" I said coldly.

"Oh Sarah, I don't know what came over me. I was just so angry all-of-a-sudden. I guess I said something to Luke, and pretty soon we were swinging at each other. I don't remember much about it, but I did talk to Luke this morning and apologized. I hope he and I can still be friends."

"What came over you, I suspect, was a whole lot of liquor!" I said in a pinched voice. "What on earth were you thinking, getting so drunk? Patrick and Cora came to see me this afternoon. They are concerned. If you keep this up, you will be sacked and then where will we be?"

"I promise, with my heart and soul I will never do this again", he said. "I swear! I love you and I never want to lose you. I promise with everything I know this will never happen again! Please, forgive me!"

I held him close for a moment and then pushed him away. "This better be the last time, James. There is a limit to what I can tolerate. And I must be careful of Emma's safety. Eat some of this stew and then go to bed. I do not want to hear any more from you tonight."

My mind was in a whirl, running back and forth and round and round. What a conundrum. I don't even know if I still love James, he treats me so badly. I also feel close to Luke and I am attracted to him. What am I to do?

A few days later, when James would be out on the range, Nat and Tom appeared at my door. I was taken by surprise and was in-the-midst of making bread. I must have looked a mess with flour all over my hands and apron.

"We came to see if you are alright," Tom said. "Should we come back? I can see this is not a good time."

"No, come on in if you do not mind a mess. Is everything OK? Is James OK?"

"We saw the fight but did not want to interfere," said Nat. "Most likely that would have just made things worse. We thought, after what has happened, you should know some things about James that he probably has not told you."

"Oh," I said. "There is so much I don't know about him. He has shared almost nothing about your family and life on your farm at home or what it was like growing up. It was clear from the time we left together he was eager to leave home. I tried to get him to talk about it, but he didn't want to."

"James has been hard to know all of his life," Nat said. "What we can tell you is that he has been moody since he was young. He used to get into fights with other kids at school a lot and was often in trouble at home. He and our father did not get along for a reason none of us understood, nor was he close to our mother. Our father would beat him with a belt, and mother would not step in to stop it."

"He is the youngest of us brothers," Tom said. "There is a big age difference between him and us. We never got along with him ourselves. Perhaps he blamed us for not standing up for him when our father came after him."

"I need to understand why James behaves so badly towards me," I said. "And towards his beautiful daughter, to his friends. He does not seem to care about who he hurts."

"Sometimes I think James was born angry," said Nat. "He has not talked to us about how he feels about you and Emma. We had both hoped that his relationship with you and getting away from home would bring him peace. I am sorry to see this apparently hasn't happened."

"We will keep you and James in our sights and keep our fingers crossed that what just happened, will be the worst!"

"Thank you for coming to see me. James may not be working here much longer if he can't get himself settled. I am grateful for whatever information and support you can give me."

Chapter Twenty-Nine

I knew I had to get away to visit Blue. I told Cora where I was going but asked her not to tell James when he got back from being out on the range if he came looking for me. I took Emma with me and hoped to return the same day.

Blue and Grace, of course, were delighted to see us. Thankfully, they did not have a busy afternoon and were able to have tea with me and talk. I told them my worries.

"One thing you can be sure of," Blue said. "If you ever need to get away for a few days, or longer, you can always stay with us. We have plenty of room at my house. We are happy to support you in any way we can."

"Thank you, Blue. I am so grateful for your friendship. And Grace. I don't know what I would do without you."

As an attempt to distract me from my troubles for a little while, Blue asked me if I would like to learn how to sew on her treadle sewing machine, a model so much more modern than my mother's.

"I would love to. My mother did teach me a little when she had time, but I never learned how to make clothes. I did manage to make a quilt of my own, however. I was quite proud of it!"

Blue also mentioned a sewing group she belongs to that meets monthly at her house in town. "The women sew quilts as well as clothing for their families. They do other kinds of handwork as well, such as knitting and crochet. It is as much a social gathering as it is a way to get some sewing done. This would be a lovely way for you to get a respite every month, and an opportunity to make new friends and learn new skills."

"I love the idea! And I want to learn to make some new clothes for myself and for Emma as she grows. And it would give me something to look forward to every month! I suppose I would have to spend the night so I could come home by daylight. And I would need to bring Emma."

"We have several bedrooms and plenty of space for you both to stay," Grace said. "There are a few other ladies who come from a distance and stay as well. Everyone brings food to share. It is wonderful fun for all of us, and a nice break from our regular duties. And, of course, if anyone needs more fabric to work with or patterns or notions, we can help them at our shop."

I was so happy I clapped my hands in pleasure, like a little girl. I need to find a way to make this work!

"That sounds like just what I need in my life! You

are so fortunate to have a home large enough to host these events. And Grace, how fortunate you are able to share such a large home with a good friend."

"It has been a wonderful outcome, in spite of very sad circumstances," said Grace. "Unfortunately, my parents do not see it that way. They expected me to marry, and in fact, they had several appropriate suitors picked out for me. But you must be aware, Sarah, that when a woman marries, everything she owns becomes the property of her husband. I was not interested in handing over my independence and whatever I might inherit to a husband. Blue felt the same and because of my decision not to marry and to live with Blue I have been cut out of my family. It has been difficult for both of us in many ways. But we live in a new age. I hope my parents will understand one day."

Our visit for the afternoon left me feeling much exhilarated and hopeful. It also gave me much to think about. I returned home just in time to make dinner, with James none the wiser. So many ideas whirling around in my head! So many new possibilities!

Chapter Thirty

Once again it was time to prepare for the annual drive of the cattle up to the train line east of Flagstaff. James made the effort to get up early, as in the year before, and put in long days preparing for the run. When the time came for the actual drive in October, he was there, beside the other hands, doing his part. I was impressed that he had been able to pull himself together for this big event. It must have been hard for him, since his drinking had become worse after the fight with Luke, but I guess Patrick's warning had made an impression.

We had a grand celebration and feast at the McBride homestead following all that hard work. As always, food and drink were offered in great abundance, but James was able to keep himself in check with the alcohol. I was much relieved. Perhaps things were going to change for the better at last.

Despite my hopes, however, James and I hardly talked when we were together. Only once did James turn to me in the night to seek comfort, but there was no warmth or joy in his touch. I cried while he slept like a baby.

Both Emma and Luna picked up on the tension in our house. Emma was fussier than usual, and Luna whined and occasionally growled at James when he was home. Once, when James aimed some sharp words at me, Luna nipped his leg. James kicked the puppy out of his way. Luna gave a sharp cry. I went quickly to pick her up and sooth her.

"James, how could you? She is just a puppy!"

"Damn dog," he said and huffed out of the house.

It was often hard to calm Emma now, and it took most of my energy to rock her until she settled down to sleep for a while. James showed no interest in her and paid her no attention. I was at my wit's end. Why can't he love her the way I do?

After the cattle drive, James seemed more and more distant. He often found reasons to go into town and usually came home in a foul mood, and drunk. When I questioned him about what had happened in town, he either said nothing or he made angry remarks about being blindsided by people he thought were his friends.

After one of these visits to town, I decided to ask him about the money we kept in a jar behind the coffee, on a shelf in the kitchen. We had agreed, after spending money on the stove and household goods, to begin putting part of James's monthly cash payment in the jar for when we needed it. That morning I had found it empty.

I knew this was not a good time to ask. He was clearly drunk, but I was upset to find our small cash reserve gone.

"James, what happened to the money we were saving in the jar? I noticed this morning that the jar was empty."

"That's my money. It is none of your business what I do with it."

"That money is half mine. I worked to earn my share, just like you did! Did you gamble it away?"

James raised his hand and slapped me hard across my face. My skin stung and I fell against the wall, bruising my shoulder. I was too shocked even to cry out. It was the first time James had ever raised a hand against me.

"You are not welcome in this house, James Parker!" I screamed when I found my voice. "Get out, now!" Luna growled and bared her teeth. Emma wailed.

"Gladly," he said, slamming the door as he left. I sank down on the floor and began to sob. Luna came to snuffle and lick my face. I put my arms around her and a little while later, I roused myself. I picked up Emma and held her till she quieted. What now?

I decided that no one must know what had happened here tonight. I was too mortified. Meanwhile, I would have to think about what I must do if it ever happens again. I had heard many stories of men who hit their wives (and worse). I was determined that I would not be such a wife. I had heard that physical abuse was apparently not grounds for divorce. If it did happen again, I would simply leave with Emma, go home to New Hampshire, if necessary. I resolved not to give in.

I began to get hints from the other hands that James's time in town did not involve just drinking and gambling, but other women. I would think if he were deliberately trying to hurt me, wouldn't he make it more obvious? Perhaps this could be an excuse for a way out of my marriage? James's brothers were sympathetic and tried to help me. Luke too. They even offered to go into town after James and check on him, but I was too proud to accept. To be honest, I am not sure I really wanted to know the truth. I declined their offers.

Chapter Thirty-One

Once again Cora and Patrick invited everyone on the ranch to a Christmas celebration. Thank goodness the bruise around my left eye had faded completely but I was not in the mood to celebrate. Emma was the one bright spot in my life, and I was proud to show her off to everyone, but otherwise kept mostly to myself. James was there, along with all the other ranch folk, but he was quiet most of the evening, hardly speaking to me or anyone else. He was hitting the booze hard.

At almost a year-old Emma was just beginning to use words (though hard to understand) and had become quite vocal, as if she had invented a private language with which she entertained herself when I was busy. She was beginning to be able to pull herself up on a chair and stand. I loved watching her gain new skills, discovering what her body could do and not do (often toppling over with surprise and giggles), and beginning to discover words had meanings. She had a bubbly laugh and everything new delighted her. She was also a very pretty child, with dark curls that bounced around her face and an active little body. I was entranced as she learned new things about her world.

For this celebration I dressed her in dark red with white leggings and a ruffled white petticoat under the dress. It was wonderful to see her become the hit of the party. She crawled vigorously from one person to another, putting her little arms up, asking to be lifted. Cliff's wife put her hand down within reach of Emma's uplifted hands and Emma grabbed hold and stood up, accompanied by shrieks of pleasure. Then, of course, others tried it until Emma tired. Cora urged James to hold her, but he just brushed her off.

Chapter Thirty-Two - 1900

Somehow, James and I made it through that winter. James mostly stayed in the barn but came up to the cabin to help shovel snow or carry coal for the stove two or three times a week, for which I was grateful. However, we rarely exchanged more than a few words. He paid no attention to Emma on these visits. At least I knew, when the snow was heavy, he was not going into town. That was my one comfort.

In January, we celebrated Emma's first birthday. What a lovely milestone. I brought her down to visit Patrick and Cora, and we had a little party. I decided to carry her over to the barn, in-spite-of the cold, to show her off to the men, since James had chosen not to acknowledge Emma's big day. Luke came over to us and asked to hold Emma. He lifted her up, twirled her around and wished her a happy birthday. The other men followed suit and cheered. Emma loved the attention. Not to be outdone in front of the other hands, James lifted her up in the air and wished her a happy first birthday. Emma laughed for each of them in her enchanting giggle. I was grateful.

James stayed with me at the cabin for a few weeks in late winter. He seemed to be more content than I had seen him in a while, for which he gave no explanation. I think he was just lonely for female company. In any case, it was nice to have a warm body with me again in our very cold bedroom. I tread very lightly when James was there, not wanting to do anything that might set him off. And for a while it worked. James was even pleasant to Emma and played with her a little. Why can't it be like this all the time?

I busied myself during the day with cooking and taking care of Emma. I still gathered the eggs and James took them down to Cora. When James was not there, I spent time reading some of the books I had borrowed from the library on a trip Cora and I had taken before the snow made it impossible to go. My favorite was Jane Eyre, by Charlotte Bronte. It was a sad but touching love story. I had also taken a copy of *Little Women*, by Louisa May Alcott. I had read it some years before and decided to read it again, as an adult. I loved Jo's courage and spunk. I also liked how determined she was to live the life she wanted to live, contrary to what was expected of women of her time. I had also found a book called *The Yellow Room*, by Charlotte Perkins Gilman. It looked to be a depressing story, and yet it intrigued me. It was about a wife completely controlled by her husband. After she has their child, he shuts her up in a room at a summer cottage that he rents, so that she can 'rest', and she eventually goes mad. I have not yet started reading it. I am not sure I can take the horror of a young mother having a mental breakdown just now.

When fair weather came, I bundled Emma up in her 'papoose' in blankets and ventured forth on snowshoes (borrowed from Cora). I did not like being cooped up in two small rooms all the time, and neither did Emma! I needed to move my body out-doors or go stir crazy. Emma seemed to enjoy our little outings too.

I often marveled at the landscape on our excursions after a new snow. There was sparkling white in all directions, broken only by the dark red house and barn, and the pine trees and mountains beyond. I wished I had a camera to capture the magic of that scene. It was dazzling. It reminded me of the days of my childhood when I would go sledding with my siblings and cousins. The hills here were not quite steep enough, but the memory was sweet.

Chapter Thirty-Three

I awoke one morning in April, with the urgent need to vomit. James was already gone. Instead of being elated, I was depressed and had a strong sense of foreboding. I determined James did not need to know yet.

I continued to be sick every morning, feeling tired and listless during the day. At a time of year when I was usually excited to see the snows diminish and spring come, I could not summon my energy and enthusiasm for the new season. To make things worse, James decided to move back down to the barn. He gave me a lame excuse of early morning chores and not wanting to disturb me.

Every day Emma had new skills and interests to show me, and I tried to engage with her. We read books together and I took her out for walks, but everything I did made me more tired and depressed.

On a sunny afternoon in early May, I took Emma down to visit Cora. She was busy in the kitchen cooking and I asked if we could visit for a while.

"Of course, child. Come in. So lovely to see you and Emma on such a beautiful day. To what do I owe the honor?"

"Cora, I need your advice. You know that my relationship with James has been rocky lately. One minute up and then back down again. I have no idea how we will be able to go on together, as things stand. Meanwhile, I have discovered I am pregnant, perhaps two months. I have said nothing to James yet, since I hardly see him, these days. Do you have any words of wisdom for me?"

Cora looked stunned, for a moment.

"You are not thinking about trying to get rid of the baby, are you?" she asked.

"Oh no, I couldn't do that! I guess I just want someone to tell me everything is going to be alright." I began to cry.

"I think you need to tell him. Perhaps that will change the way he feels about you and your marriage."

"Perhaps."

"In any case, whatever happens between you and James, you will still have another sweet baby to look forward to and take care of. We will happily support you and the baby. Please, just don't do anything rash."

By now, the snow was mostly gone and the track through the grass to Flagstaff was passable. I decided one day in early May to borrow a wagon and horse without telling James to go to Flagstaff to see Blue and

Grace. I took Emma with me and our rifle (just in case).

It felt wonderful to be out in the spring air. There was a slight breeze, and the wildflowers were budding and a few already in bloom. I could smell their sweet aroma. My spirits began to lift as I looked forward to being on my own with Emma for a few hours and seeing my dearest friends.

As always, Grace and Blue greeted me with enthusiasm, and were delighted to see Emma.

"Let me know when you are ready to join our sewing bee," Blue said. "Now that it is easier to travel, more women have joined since we started up again in April."

"I would love to, but my life with James is very unsteady right now and..." I surprised myself by bursting into tears.

"Oh, Sarah," Grace said, putting her arm around my shoulders. "What is it? Let us help if we can."

I sobbed. "I am pregnant!"

"Well, that should be good news!" Blue said. "Is there something wrong?"

"I don't know," I said, trying to get myself under control. "I just have the strangest feeling, like something bad is going to happen."

"I have heard from some of the women in the sewing group, that sometimes they feel like you do in the early months and then everything works out fine after the baby is born. Perhaps that is what is happening to you." Blue gave me a hug.

"What does James think about having another child?" Grace asked. "Perhaps a boy, this time?"

"I have not told him yet. I know I must, and soon, before I start to show. I don't know how he will take it. This is not a good time to ask him about the sewing group. I hope I can attend soon. Thank you again for your friendship and support!"

I returned home before James came back from the barn, for which I was grateful. I resolved to talk to him after dinner if he was in a good mood.

When James returned, I had dinner ready and waiting, baked potatoes with butter, stewed mixed vegetables with shredded cheese, and baked apples. He seemed to be in a tolerable mood, so after dinner I plucked up my courage.

"James. I need to tell you something important. Do you remember when you stayed with me for a few weeks last winter? How close we were? Well, we will have another baby in December or January. Perhaps a boy this time!"

James looked blank for a moment. "Are you sure?" he asked.

"Yes, I am sure. Wouldn't it be wonderful to have a son? You could teach him all the things you know about ranching, riding horses and being a cowboy!"

"As you say, my dear." He got up from the table,

knocking over the chair in the process, and went out. I did not see him again for several days.

Chapter Thirty-Four

I threw myself into spring planting, after the men had dug and prepared the soil. Julia and I spent several days planting a variety of vegetables: several types of summer squash along with our usual tomatoes, beans, cucumbers, and some greens we had not tried before. We decided to try several varieties of winter squash, and of course carrots, beets, and turnips. It looked like it would be a good year for the garden, if not for me.

When the 'monsoons' arrived in late July and through August, we celebrated. The garden was like a sponge, soaking up every drop while every day the plants filled out and grew taller. Best of all, the water 'tank' filled up for the first time since it was built. What a blessing! However, James did not come to see me and Emma, not even to help carry coal for the cookstove and I resolved not to go after him.

I was surprised one afternoon when Nat showed up while I was in the garden weeding.

"I hope you do not mind, Sarah," he said, by way of greeting. "James told me and Tom that you were expecting another baby. I just wanted to stop by and congratulate you and see how you are doing."

"That is kind of you, Nat. It would be nice if James showed me the same courtesy. He appears to have no interest in me or the new baby." I stopped in my work to wipe my brow of sweat.

"I have never seen him behave this way before. I almost do not recognize him," Nat said.

"I appreciate you stopping by Nat. Just tell James…" I searched for the words. "Just tell him I am doing fine on my own. Thank you for your concern." I turned my back before Nat could see my tears.

Julia and I harvested a bounty of vegetables in September and spent many hours, with Cora's help, canning, drying, preserving, and storing as much as we could against the winter. Braided ropes of onions and garlic hung from the rafters in my kitchen. Cora was happy to receive as much as I could give her, and the chickens enjoyed heaps of extra greens. Everything else went into the compost pile I had started the year before. I was exhausted and my back hurt so much I finally allowed myself to take a much-needed rest. Julia took Emma down to the ranch house so I could sleep for a while. What a luxury in the middle of the day.

I awoke with a start to find James standing over me. Luna was growling softly.

"James. What are you doing here in the middle of

the day? Is something wrong?" I sat up hurriedly and pulled my shawl around me. A shiver ran up my spine.

"Where is Emma? Why are you sleeping in the middle of the day?" he said, roughly.

"Emma is with Julia and Cora down at the ranch house. I was simply exhausted after putting up our harvest for the winter with Julia, and my back has been paining me. You haven't told me why you are here."

"Nat told me he had stopped by to see how you were doing a while back. He said he thought you were working too hard in your condition. I decided I should come see for myself. Looks like maybe Nat was right."

"So nice of you to come check on me." I said with annoyance. "Good thing we are all done for the year and I can go back to doing nothing all day. And, by-the-way, Emma and I are both doing very well, thanks so much for asking. Now, if you do not mind, I am going down to the ranch house to see Cora and bring Emma home." I walked past James and out the door, calling Luna to come with me. I did not look back.

Chapter Thirty-Five – Fall 1900

Soon preparations for the annual cattle drive began again, although I had little to do with it except to prepare food for the celebration. I made a large stew of chicken and a medley of vegetables with biscuits. Julia helped carry everything down while I carried Emma.

I did not see James again until the night of the celebration meal after the successful drive. By then I had a significant bump under my blouse, and I received many inquiries into my health and that of the baby, as well as good wishes and congratulations from those who had not seen me for a while. James finally approached me to ask after me and the baby, as well as Emma. I could see looks going back and forth between the hands and the others, but that did not bother me. I had long since assumed everyone on the ranch knew we were not living together.

"We are all fine, James. Emma, me, and the baby. Thanks for asking." I turned away from him and spoke to Patrick, who happened to be closest.

Patrick whispered softly to me with his back turned to James. "Are you really fine, Sarah? Something isn't right. I hope you can tell Cora and me if we can help in any way."

I gave him a big smile and said loud enough for James to hear, "Thank you for your well wishes, Patrick. I am much obliged." I saw James headed over to the table that held the beer, and I spoke again, softly, to Patrick. "All is not as I would wish it, but at least my health is good. Thank you for your concern."

Luke was standing nearby and raised his eyebrows to me in question. I smiled and nodded to him but moved away when I saw James returning with a beer in his hand.

One day in early November, James offered to take me into town. I was happy that he had offered and looked forward to our trip and to seeing Blue and Grace, since snow would be coming soon. I decided to leave Emma with Cora, who adored her and was happy to have a whole afternoon playing with her.

James dropped me off at Blue's shop and went to get the things we needed for the chickens, (he said). I was suspicious about where he was going (to see a woman, gamble with his friends, drink?) but said nothing.

As always, it was wonderful to see Blue and Grace. I was glad to have an opportunity to confide in them.

We talked about a new maternity outfit for me,

and Blue took measurements, as before, but that was just a pretext for me to be there to visit with my closest friends.

When James came to get me, it was clear he was very drunk and in a foul mood. He was slurring his words and his eyes were very dark. His heavy breathing chilled me. He is scaring me. He is looking right through me as if I were not here. Who is this man? I stepped back.

"James," I said with a tremor in my voice, "Blue has invited me to stay here for a few days to help them in the shop. I will find a way back to the ranch by the end of the week, so you do not have to make a special trip to fetch me. I want to help them with a project they are working on." I tried to hide my shaking hands.

James became increasingly angry at this. "No, you will come home with me now! I need you home and Emma needs her mother!"

Both Grace and Blue stepped in front of me. Blue said. "We would like to have Sarah stay with us for a few days. We have a big commission to work on and Sarah can be helpful in the shop."

Grace was blunt. "You are very drunk and in no condition to drive Sarah home," she said.

For a moment I thought James might strike Grace. I flinched.

"Get out of my way," James said with a snarl. "Sarah is my wife, and she will do as I say. You are just a couple whores. I do not want my wife associating with you!" James turned to me. "Come on," he said sharply. He grabbed my arm and pulled me towards the door.

I knew enough not to push him when he was in a mood like this. He insisted and I gave in.

We passed through the outskirts of town, then the scrub pines. There were no words between us as the wagon plodded along the dirt track through the long grass. As the silence stretched on, I became increasingly uneasy. James's face became darker, and his body sat stiffly on the wagon seat. I sat as far away from him as I could and cradled my round belly with my hands.

Half-way back to the ranch, James suddenly stopped the wagon. He hissed these words, "I know you are carrying a bastard child!"

"What are you talking about?" I asked. "What would make you think such a thing?"

"I see the way he looks at you, all moon eyed, like an elk in rut."

"James, Luke is my friend. I would never..."

"So," he slurred. "it is Luke's? Are you meeting him in Flagstaff? Is that why you want to stay with Blue?"

"I have never been with Luke! Why would you even think that? The baby is yours!"

"You are lying!"

"Oh James, don't you remember when you stayed with me last winter? How sweet that was? That is when I conceived this baby."

"I don't believe you! If you want to stay in Flagstaff so badly, go! Get out!"

"What do you mean?" I asked.

"Get out now!" he shouted. "You and your bastard. Go back to Flagstaff to your lover! How could you betray me like this?"

"I have not betrayed you," I cried. "I do not know what you mean!"

James slapped me and pushed me hard off the wagon seat. When I tried to hang on, begging him to stop, he kicked me in the chest and abdomen, again and again, with his heavy boots until I fell, with a scream, onto the ground. I landed on my back and could not breathe at first. As I watched the wagon disappear, I tried to cry out, but of course, no one could hear me. The pain was excruciating in my chest and my belly. I felt wetness between my legs and my head throbbed.

I have been abandoned! No one can hear me! I am dying. My baby!

The next thing I remember were voices and arms lifting me up. I looked for James, but he was not there. Luke was holding me gently, and James's brothers, Nat, and Tom, were bending over me. Then I saw Cora and wondered why she might be there. I was totally disoriented. Is this a bad dream? I want to wake up!

I must have passed out again and had no recollection of the men bringing me home or what happened after that. When I finally came to, I found myself dressed in a clean nightgown, resting in my own bed. I felt someone near me. She took my hand and brought her face close to mine.

"I am so sorry, Sarah," she whispered. "Your baby boy was dead when I delivered him. He was gravely injured-there was no way to save him. You have lost a great deal of blood and may have some cracked or broken ribs. I have made tea for you-it will help with the pain and help begin the healing."

"Cora, is that you??"

"Yes, Sarah."

"What has happened? Why are you here?" Not my baby? Tears were streaming down my face.

"Easy, now, Sarah. You have had an accident. You have been injured and lost a lot of blood. Now drink some of this tea. You will feel better."

"Thank you, Cora, I am beholden to you," I whispered. I slept again.

The next day, Luke came to visit me. Cora was still there, clucking over me like a mother hen. Julia was looking after Emma and Luna, both of whom wanted to know what had happened to me. I was feeling better but was exhausted and sore. My mind seemed clearer, and I was beginning to understand what James had done.

"The men were worried when James returned home without you," Luke told me. "James said you wanted to stay in Flagstaff with your friends for a few days. We didn't buy his story considering the condition and mood he was in when he got back. We decided we had better check along the wagon track to Flagstaff.

"When we found you, you were unconscious and covered in blood. We decided we better get Cora to help you." Then, softly, in my ear, Luke said "Sarah, I am so sorry you lost the baby." When I tried to move a little the pain was so sharp it took my breath away. "Don't try to move, you may have some broken ribs." He took my hand and held it gently.

"Where is James?" I asked in a whisper.

"He is roped and tied in one of the stalls until we can decide what to do with him," Luke said. "He does not remember anything about what he did. He is in a pretty sorry state."

Cora brought me more of her tea and gently spooned some of it into my mouth. It was soothing and I could feel its warmth spreading through me. I felt sleepy.

Later Cora returned, this time with Patrick. The smell coming from the dish Cora carried made me suddenly hungry, and I realized I could not remember when I last ate anything.

"I brought you some rice and beans with shredded cheese. I hope you can eat some-you need to get your strength back," said Cora. She bent close to me and kissed my cheek. "I am so sorry this has happened to you."

"How are you feeling?" asked Patrick gruffly."
It looked like he was fighting tears. "We should have
been more aware–I am so sorry. James will pay for this;
you can be sure."

"What will happen to him?" I asked.

"That will be up to the sheriff in Flagstaff when
he gets there. His brothers have offered to come with
me when we bring him in. What a bloody business. I
never imagined it would come to this. Meanwhile, my
dear, as we have told you before, you will have a place
here as long as you want, so don't worry none about
that".

"Thank you, Patrick. I am so grateful for all you
have done. I will try to make up for this somehow."

"Don't be silly, child. This was all James's
doing!"

Cora put some of the savory smelling food in a
bowl with a spoon and brought it to me. I tried to sit up
a little so I could eat. My ribs pained me, but with Cora
and Patrick's help, I was able to raise up on the pillows
enough to swallow a few bites. It was delicious and I
began to revive a little.

Strangely, I did not yet mourn my unborn child.
In fact, I felt oddly numb. My heart was empty. A boy,
Cora had whispered to me. Did that really happen to
me or did I dream it? I was too tired to think. I slept
long and deep, knowing I was surrounded by people
who loved me, and that I was safe.

PART III

Fall 1900 – Spring 1902

Chapter Thirty-Six

While I convalesced through that long winter, I had plenty of time to think, with little to do except take care of Emma and Luna. The one thing I was sure of was that I was safe. In October, James had been taken by Patrick, with Nat's and Tom's assistance, to the jail in Flagstaff. I did not yet know what would happen to him, but I did know, for sure, that, at least for the time being, he could no longer come near me or Emma. I was also relieved that I no longer had to worry about what kind of mood James might be in when he came home, how drunk he might be, or how he might criticize me for every little thing I did. It has been a long time since I have felt so free of fear.

In January Emma had a birthday, but I hardly noticed. I was grateful when Cora and Julia appeared with a small gift for Emma and a treat for me to mark another year in Emma's life. She was two years old! Life goes on, whether you will it or not.

I still did not yet mourn or regret the loss of my unborn son. I found that strange. However, if he had lived, he would likely have been severely disabled from his injuries, and another reminder of what James did to me. Cora and Patrick had buried him in a quiet spot near the garden and laid a stone to mark the tiny grave. I did not visit it. I put him out of my mind and moved on.

As I became stronger, I gradually resumed my duties with Julia's help and encouragement. I became more active in Emma's life, delighting with each new step and little accomplishment that she was eager to show me. I remembered well how distant and unavailable my mother had become after my father's death and I vowed I would not be like that for my loving and sensitive daughter.

I baked bread and made stews, scrubbed the floors, cleaned the kitchen, washed all the linens, and organized my little cabin. Staying busy helped keep my mind clear and I gradually began to feel whole again.

Together, Julia and I got the garden planted when the weather warmed, and Julia took the daily collection of eggs to her mother. Emma continued to grow and was now 2 ½ years old. I could hardly believe it! She delighted in helping me find hidden eggs and was quite pleased with herself when she succeeded. She did much to raise my spirits. Luna too–her irrepressible joy at simply being alive was a tonic for my heart. I took pleasure in watching Luna and Emma play together and run through the long grass, barking, and laughing.

Luke visited almost every day after his work was done to "check on me," he said. I was grateful for his visits. I would make coffee and slice up a loaf of freshly baked bread and we would sit and talk outside if it were a fair day, or in the kitchen if not. We shared stories about our lives before we met, and I finally had a chance to ask him about his life before coming to the ranch.

"Cora told me some months ago that you showed up one day at the ranch, riding bare-back on a pony, looking for work. She said you were young, very thin, and that you brought only the clothes on your back. She did not know where you had come from and didn't want to pry, but as a mother, she knew you needed to be fed and cared for. She also told me she was glad she and Patrick had taken a chance on you. You grew up to be a fine ranch hand, one of the best they have ever had, she told me. She is very fond of you." Luke grinned at that.

"Patrick and Cora have been good to me. I owe them so much for taking in a castaway," he said. "I imagine they must have been pretty surprised when I showed up out of nowhere. I must have been desperate to think I could show up with nothing and expect to be fed and housed by strangers. White strangers. In the beginning I worked in the stable, mucking out stalls and pitching hay. I had to prove myself before I was able to earn any money for my work. I was just grateful for being fed and having a safe place to sleep. And, unlike the other hands, I did not spend my pay when I had any. I hid it, saving for the future."

"So, where did you come from? Before coming to the ranch, I mean. I want to know everything about you." I blushed and Luke smiled, shyly.

"I lived in a village on the Navajo reservation, northeast of here. I never met my father, but my mother told me he was a white man who rode through the area, one day, with a group of rowdy cowboys.

They had been drinking. My mother told me she was working in her garden when he found her. Apparently 'Indian squaws', as the white men liked to call them, were fair game at the time. She had nothing good to say about him except that he made me, and she loved me. She never even knew his name."

"How awful for your mother," I said. "I am happy that she loved and raised you, when she could have easily cast you away."

"Yes. Growing up, I was very conscious that I was mixed blood. My mother tried to protect me, but the other children made fun of me, and I was not fully accepted by my elders. About that time, white soldiers began taking children away from their families in many villages, to send away to boarding schools, where they stayed until they were eighteen. Some never saw their families again.

"Children were taught hiding games by their parents to protect them. Later the soldiers took children by force, sometimes killing anyone who stood in the way. They took me when I was nine. I remember trying to hold onto my mother's hand and watching her cry as I left with a group of other children from my village. It broke my heart." Luke wiped tears from his eyes but managed to go on. I put my hand on his arm.

"At the school I was taken to, they cut off all my hair and took away my clothes, clothing that my mother had made for me. All the children were dressed the same and had no hair. I felt terrible shame when my hair was cut off. I was no longer a brave warrior. We all became 'nobodies.'. We were given new American names and we were not allowed to speak our own languages. Children came from many different tribes and spoke differently from each other, but if any of us tried to speak to another child who spoke our own language, we would be beaten. We were forced to learn the white man's language. Every night I cried in my bed, missing my mother, and hating the way we were being treated."

"Oh, how terrible for you and the other children! I never heard of that being done before. It is shocking! How did you manage to survive?"

"I dreamed every night and every day of finding a way to escape. I focused on that and did what I was told."

"Is 'Luke' the name they gave you?"

"No. I could not stand being called by the name they gave me. I chose the name 'Luke' after I left. I saw it written in a bible they made us read."

"So, what happened? How did you get away?"

"When I was older, I worked in the gardens where we grew vegetables to feed everyone. It was hard work, but at least we were outdoors. The fresh air and the exercise felt good and sometimes we could sneak something to eat. There was a high fence all around the garden area and there were always guards watching us all the time. I got into trouble several times when I was trying to scout a way out. Eventually, I spotted a weak point in the fence and one night, when there was no moon, I was able to sneak out of the dormitory and slip away. I ran for several miles before finding a place I could hide and rest for a while. Then I kept going until daylight. I found another hiding place in a small barn, and the next night I stole a pony and kept going. I wanted to go home but I did not know where I was and, besides, that would probably be the first place they would look for me. I was scared and hungry. I just wanted to get as far away from that so-called school as I could."

"How long has it been since you last saw your mother?"

"More than fifteen years, I think. I lost track of time. I still miss her greatly and did send word to her that I had found work on a ranch and that she should not worry for me. I asked her not to try to find me–I did not want anyone from that school to come after me. Perhaps I will try to find her again, one day."

"How sad, Luke," I said. "But you are now your own man, and you should be proud of that! You have made a successful life for yourself here. But I do hope you can find your mother one day and let her know she raised a fine son."

I had told Luke about what my early life was like. He understood my grief over the death of my father and my bond with my mother when I was young. He tried to understand what it was like to be living with a second family and never feeling quite a part of it. We certainly came from totally different worlds. But more and more I felt the two of us becoming closer. Each of us had wounds that needed to heal.

Meanwhile, my thoughts kept turning to my family back home and I determined I must go. I had so many questions, now that James was out of my life (at least I hoped so) and I did not know yet how to proceed, in my current circumstances. My heart is here, on the ranch. I love my life here, my work and my friends. I feel free to be my own person here. But would I be able to get legally separated from James? Is it possible to get a divorce? I would not be able to bear it If I can't be released from the disaster that was my marriage. I need to make sure James can never hurt me or Emma ever again.

Mama and Ben will know how to advise me. It would be a visit only. I would return to my friends and my life here. There is so much here for me that I could not have with my family back in New Hampshire. And how can I leave so many kind people behind? Julia, Blue, Grace, Patrick, and Cora. And Luke.

Chapter Thirty-Seven

"Julia," I asked one day after we had spent the afternoon planting and weeding. "How would you like an adventure that would take you all the way across the country on a train to where I grew up in New Hampshire? You would be able to meet my family. I need to go, and I will need help with Emma, and I want to take Luna, as well. Of course, I would pay your way."

"Oh my! Yes!" Julia said with glee. "I would love to go. I have never been anywhere but here and have never been on a train! Of course," she said, sobering, "I will need to get permission from my parents."

To my delight, and Julia's, both Cora and Patrick loved the idea.

"This will be a wonderful opportunity for Julia to learn so many new things! New places to experience, new people to meet, strange foods to try," Patrick laughed at that one.

"There is nothing like travel, especially if you have never been beyond your own back yard, to widen your horizons," Cora said. "This is an amazing offer! I have an idea for a way you can make the trip even more meaningful and interesting. Take a notebook with you and write a journal about what you see and do. You do not have to include things like changing diapers, but you know what I mean. You can collect souvenirs or mementos to add to your account. What do you think, Julia?"

"I think that is a great idea. I could make a scrapbook and write stories about what I see and who I meet."

"Exactly. Then you can entertain everyone here when you get home so they can enjoy your trip vicariously!"

And so, I set my trip east in motion. We would go in the fall after harvest.

August 1901

Dearest Mama,

I have decided to come home for a while. I have lots of things to think about regarding my future. I will tell you more when I come. Meanwhile I would like to stay with you and Ben and the family while I think about what comes next in my life. Please do not think badly of me. I need your support right now. I will send a telegram when I leave to let you know when to expect us. I will be bringing my daughter, your granddaughter, Emma, who is 2 ½ years old, my friend, Julia, and my sweet dog, Luna.

I will see you all soon—I have missed you so!

Much love to each of you.
Sarah

Part IV

October 1901 to June 1902

Chapter Thirty-Eight

Once again, I was standing at a train station waiting for the train to arrive. How different my going would be this time. Julia and Emma were beside themselves with excitement and Luna, too. Blue was there as well and appeared to be fighting tears. I put my arms around her.

"Please do not weep, Blue. You have been my best friend and the sister I never had. I could not have survived the past months without you and Grace. It will only be a few months until I return. Meanwhile, please write to me."

"My heart goes with you," she whispered. "I will write to you faithfully until your return."

I had said my goodbyes to Patrick and Cora at the ranch and promised to come back. Patrick gave me two months-worth of James's cash stipend to cover our expenses for the trip, in addition to paying for his daughter.

"Please, Dear Sarah, come back to us," Cora said tearfully. "You are an important part of our ranch family. Little Emma too. This place will not be the same without you.

Patrick said gruffly, "You will be greatly missed, you and Emma. I will even miss your crazy dog Luna!" I could see he was trying to make light of our parting, but he had tears in his eyes. I reached up on my toes and kissed his cheek.

"I don't know what to say to you," I said. "Your friendship and support are everything to me. I will be back, I hope, in the spring."

Luke drove us into town with all our gear. He was quiet on the way while Julia had a thousand questions. Luke and I had talked for a long time the day before, walking near the cabin with Emma and Luna running on ahead through the golden grass.

"I wish you were not going, but I understand your need to go," Luke had said. His eyes glittered, and he looked away. I took his hand.

"You know I have much to sort out and I think my family, especially my mama, can help me decide what is best for me and Emma."

"When will you come back? I am afraid of losing you." His voice broke.

"I don't know. My intention is to stay through the winter and return here in the spring."

"And if you decide to stay?"

"Please, Luke. I need time to think. I do not know what the future holds."

"I need you to know before you go how I feel about you." He took my hand, and we stood close together. "I have loved you for a long time. I have not wanted to intrude or to push you." He looked away. "I just want you to know how I feel." His voice cracked.

"I know, Luke," I said gently. "I have been able to feel it. You have helped sustain me through some truly terrible times. I love you too, but I am not yet free."

"I hope you will write to me. I will wait for you until you know what you want to do."

"I will. I promise." I whispered.

When the train finally arrived and rolled to a stop, I gave Luke a quick kiss on the cheek and Blue as well. Luke gave Julia a hug.

"Be good," he whispered in her ear. "Bring her back to me and yourself as well."

Julia went up the steps first, and I lifted Emma to the top of the step into Julia's arms. I followed with Luna on a short lead. Luna was nervous about the steps and all the unfamiliar noises and smells, but we finally boarded and found our seats. I had considered leaving Luna behind, but Emma cried so piteously, I relented. I was glad she was coming with us. She was a comforting presence.

How different this was from my journey West, just three short years ago. This time I knew what to expect and was able to navigate the changes in Chicago and Boston without assistance. Julia was wonderful with Emma, who, to her great credit (and my great relief) did not fuss much except at bedtime. Luna was a handful, but between Julia and me, we were able to get her outside when the train stopped, and she mostly lay on the floor between us. I had brought food for each of us, and we were able to purchase drinks and sandwiches when we wanted to, thanks to Patrick. This trip was far easier than I had anticipated, and I was grateful.

Chapter Thirty-Nine

When we finally arrived at the train station in my little village in New Hampshire, we had quite the reception waiting for us. Mama and Ben, of course, Jacob and Alice and their little boys, (one a brand-new infant), and my four younger half- siblings. Oh my, we had a crowd! It was hard to know whom to hug first, but Mama immediately swept me into her arms.

"Welcome home, my dearest daughter," she whispered, as she kissed my cheek. Her face was wet with tears. Ben, too, gave me a warm bear hug. Happy tears filled my eyes as well.

"I am so glad you are home again where you belong, Sarah." Ben said. "We have all missed you so much!" Then Jacob took me in his arms and whirled me around, right off my feet. Oh my, it really feels like I am wanted and welcome here!

Then so many introductions. I met Jacob's Alice and their adorable little boys. Charlie, just starting to walk, tried to hide behind Alice but peeked out at me in wonder. Alice carried the new baby in her arms.

Julia was holding one of Emma's hands as she walked unsteadily towards my family. Luna was already busy introducing herself to everyone, wagging her whole body with excitement.

"This sweet little girl is Emma your granddaughter," I said as I made the introduction, "and this is my friend Julia, Patrick, and Cora's eldest child. She has been an enormous help with the baby and with Luna on this long journey. I see you have already met Luna!" I said, laughing. Emma was braver than her little cousin and allowed herself to be kissed and hugged by her grandparents and Uncle Jacob. Plenty of time to meet the rest of the family, we agreed.

The day was fair and warm, and the leaves were only just beginning to change color. It was my favorite kind of New England early fall day, one thing I had missed sorely in Arizona. We all walked from the train station to my parent's large home nearby, where we were welcomed by Gladys and Sallie Mae and a huge spread for a late lunch/early dinner. I was overwhelmed and could not help but weep as I stepped up onto the wide verandah and we all entered the house. I am home! I am truly home. I could not hold back the tears that flowed at that moment.

I asked, later, if Julia and Luna could stay in one bedroom and Emma and me in another but somehow, during the night we all ended up together in the same bed and it felt right. Breakfast, of course, was a major production. Sallie Mae outdid herself to make sure we were well fed, including Luna.

"Miss Sarah," asked Julia, "who are all the people in this house, I mean besides your mother and Mr.

Stone?"

"The children are my younger sisters and my brother (I decided not to try to explain half-siblings just yet). My sister Becky is sixteen. She is the taller girl with sandy colored hair. Lyddie is my second sister. She is the one with braids. She is fourteen. Then comes Benny–he is twelve. He is likely with Ben right now in the workshop. My youngest sister, Maggie, is about nine, if I remember correctly. We did have quite a houseful when Jacob and I were still living here!

"And who are the two other ladies?" Julia asked.

"The one with red hair is named Gladys. She is from Ireland, and has a lovely accent. Ben hired her after Maggie was born to help with the children and to manage the house. Mama was starting her business then and needed extra help.

"Sallie Mae came all the way here from the south with her family after the Civil War. She was just a little girl when they came here. She grew up to be an excellent cook and we hired her to take care of the chickens, food shopping and preparing the meals. She is also a wonderful seamstress, and she helps mama keep up with all her designing and making of quilts."

I think Julia was totally overwhelmed by the house, the huge breakfast, the whole idea of being served by a woman who was black and a servant. I was not used to this treatment either since I had left home. It felt strange to be waited on and not have any chores to do.

When Julia asked me to show her and Emma

the 'necessary' out back, I took her to the big indoor bathroom on the main floor. Her mouth dropped open when I turned on the faucet for the sink and hot water came out after running the cold. The porcelain bathtub was enormous compared to the metal wash tubs we were used to, and Julia jumped back when I showed her how to flush the toilet.

It was all too much for both Emma and Julia. We soon decided to take a walk outside to get some fresh air and visit the lake across the road from my parent's house. Luna, of course, was thrilled and immediately rushed into the water. I found a stick and threw it for her, and she happily swam after it and brought it back. That was a fun game for a while!

"I used to swim in this lake when I was growing up," I said to the girls, "and we went boating together. In the wintertime, when the lake was frozen, we would go skating from one end of the lake to the other if we were lucky enough to have the lake freeze solid before the snows came. We would hold hands and make a line as we skated as fast as we could and then the person on the end of the line would suddenly stop and we would "crack the whip"! It was great fun. Sometimes you could hear a great booming sound coming from under the ice. Then we moved quickly towards the shore in case the ice cracked.

"The house we are staying in is where I lived when I was older. When I was a little girl, I lived on a farm a few miles from here. We skated on the pond there, too, if the ice froze before the snow came. We also made holes in the ice to catch fish. It is where your Uncle Jacob and Aunt Alice live now with their little boys. We will go visit them soon."

"I have never seen a lake before," Julia said, "only a river. This lake is so big I can't even see to the end of it! How could it freeze enough so you could stand on the water? What is skating?" I laughed as she asked question after question about this strange place.

"I really like your parents," Julia said. "And your sisters. But I don't think I could live in such a big house," said Julia. "Too many rooms and some of them, like the room we slept in last night, are high up, not on the ground like my house at home." I had to agree, though I did not say so out loud. I don't know if I could ever get used to living in a house like that again. It is too grand, and I don't feel like I belong here, and being waited on by servants feels uncomfortable. My cozy two-room cabin is fine with me! It fits me. It is mine and it is home. No one needs to wait on me!

I took the two girls and Luna on a long walk around our little village, then back to the house. I wanted some time to speak with Mama and Ben. I asked my sister Becky to take Julia and Emma up to the playroom on the third floor. Lyddie and Maggie, my younger sisters, wanted to go too. Gladys joined them as well. I hoped they would entertain Emma for a while.

I went to the drawing room to see if Mama and Ben were there. Ben was, and I decided to sit with him for a while before searching out my mother in her sewing room upstairs.

I think Ben was as nervous as I was. We both started talking at once, and then we laughed. Our laughter broke the tension.

"I am so happy to see you home again," Ben said. "Your mother has missed you terribly. We all have. For a long time, your sisters and Benny have been asking when you would be coming home, but we had no answers. It is wonderful to see you. You look beautiful and all grown up!" Ben hugged me and again I could see tears in his eyes.

"I am glad to be here also, Ben. Thank you for such a warm reception. I did not know how you would feel after the way I left."

"Nonsense," Ben said gruffly. "You are our beloved daughter This is where you belong! I think I understand much more than you realize why you left. You probably do not remember the stories I told you and Jacob when you were little, about how I grew up on a French-Canadian farm and left home without a backward look when I was the same age as you were when you left. I was the youngest of thirteen and had no prospects. I even went so far as to change my name when I moved to northern New Hampshire to work as a lumberjack. I was so angry I did not want to ever see my parents again."

"I was also a hot-blooded young man in those days, long before I met your mother. I can certainly understand James wanting to be with a beautiful girl like you, and you were so young and inexperienced! I am so grateful we did not lose you!"

"I did not know about how you left home, Ben. Thank you for sharing that with me. It helps to know you do understand. I want to hear more of this story, sometime, if you are willing to tell it."

"Of course," Ben said.

"So much has happened to me since I left home, and I have a lot to tell you and Mama. I have a lot to think over and I am hoping you and Mama can help me sort things out. There are many things I wish to share with you, many happy stories, and some," my voice cracked, "some too hard to talk about yet."

"I want to hear whatever you want to tell us, in your own time. There is no hurry."

"Thank you, Ben. And thank you for not judging me. I want to see Mama now–is she upstairs?"

When I went up to Mama's sewing room, I could hear giggling coming from the playroom on the third floor. It was a happy sound.

Mama was delighted to see me. It was almost as if she had been waiting for me. Again, there was awkwardness between us, but when the conversation finally started, it was like a dam broke. Words poured out of each of us. I was reminded of the far away time when I was perhaps 16 when I had sat in this very room and asked her a lot of questions about my father and Ben and how I fit into the family. It was almost as if no time had passed.

"Oh, Mama–the ranch is so amazing! I just love being there. The family we work for are wonderful– they treat us like members of their family. My life with Emma is so full and exciting. She is the joy of my life! I have free reign over developing the garden and taking care of the chickens, so I feel like I am quite independent. It is the perfect arrangement, in some ways."

"It sounds wonderful, dear. Jacob told us quite a lot about what your life was like out there. He was really taken with the beauty of the place and how friendly everyone was. He adored meeting his little niece, Emma! It is so wonderful for us to finally meet her in person!"

"Oh, Mama–I do need to talk to you and Ben about James. That is the one very dark part of my life at present. I am just not quite ready yet."

Mama had been working on an intricately designed quilt in many colors, which she put aside so we could talk.

"Mama, I am so grateful you and Ben are not judging me for what I did to you. You know from my letters how sorry I am for the way I treated you! I just really need your support, now."

"Of course, sweetheart. Ben and I will help you any way we can when you are ready to tell us what has happened and what you need."

"Perhaps," I said, "after dinner the three of us can talk. Tomorrow I want to take Emma and Julia out to see Jacob and Alice and possibly stay there for a few days."

"That sounds like a fine idea, Sarah."

After a pause, I said "Mama, this quilt top you are working on is really beautiful! I love the variety of colors."

"It is a scrap quilt–I have so many left-over pieces from all the other quilts I have made. This is a wonderful way to use some of them. I have finally worked out the design but have not yet written up any instructions. Do you really like it? "

"Yes, it is lovely."

"You may have it when it's finished if you like. It will keep you warm in the cold NH winters."

"Oh Mama–thank you! That is very generous! I will treasure it! I just am not sure what my future holds yet, and Julia must eventually return home."

"Of course, dear. We will talk about all that when the time is right."

I could hear the children descending the stairs, preceded by their laughter. I went downstairs to greet them.

"Mama," Emma said happily, "look at this doll that Becky and Lyddie gave me! "Emma held it up so I could see every detail. I recognized the doll. It had once been mine! She had a lovely porcelain face with a swirl of fine dark hair surrounding it, and she was wearing a pretty outfit made of dark green taffeta, with matching hat and dainty shoes of white leather. "They said I could keep her! I think I will name her Blue." There were looks of surprise from the other children.

"Why would you name her Blue?" asked Becky.

"Mama has a friend named Blue. This is my friend Blue."

I gave Emma a hug and welcomed her doll Blue into our family.

After dinner, another grand affair with too much food and ceremony, the children got ready for bed. Gladys promised baths for the children and then bedtime stories. Julia joined them. Ben, Mama, and I went to the drawing room for tea and to talk.

Chapter Forty

I fiddled with my handkerchief, not quite knowing how to begin, and took a deep breath.

"It is a long story. Please bear with me. James and I were so happy together in the beginning and excited to start our new lives in a new world. We each found jobs that suited us as soon as we arrived, and we love living and working on the ranch. We were lucky to find the perfect situation so quickly and we were so in love, everything seemed magical. But I was with child right away, and James was clearly not happy about that. I loved the idea of being a mother, but it was difficult to understand why expecting a child should upset James." I paused for a moment to clear my throat, then went on.

"Our first year together was sometimes good and he did help me when it was time for Emma to come, but after that he showed little interest in her or in me. He was drinking quite a lot with the men, and that just got worse. Often, he went into town, presumably to gamble but I do not know what else. I think I did not want to know! Eventually he was drinking a great deal and got into fights with some of the hands. It began to look like our employer, Mr. McBride might fire him. However, Mr. McBride, Patrick as he prefers to be called, told me I was always welcome there, me and Emma, even if James was let go." I began to cry.

"It is OK, Sarah," Ben said gently. "You do not have to tell us more until you are ready."

"No, I have started. Let me finish," I said, wiping my eyes. "James used to take me into town to get supplies. He did not like me driving the wagon there by myself. I made friends with a wonderful woman named Blue, and her business partner Grace who are dress makers there. They own their own shop, much like Aunt Rebecca. I was able to talk to them when things got bad, and they offered me a place to stay if I ever needed to get away.

"I became pregnant again about a year after Emma was born. James had been mostly staying in the barn at the time but came and stayed with me for a few days in the winter to help with chores. We became close again during that time. He was angry when he found out about the baby and did not want to believe the baby was his. When I was well along in my pregnancy, seven months I think, he offered to take me into town again so I could visit my friends and he could get supplies.

"When he arrived at Blue's shop to take me home, he was drunk and extremely angry. He would not tell me why. I did not want to go with him, but he insisted. I will spare you some of the details, but on the way back to the ranch he literally kicked me off the wagon and abandoned me. In doing this he killed our unborn baby, and I was severely injured. James is now in jail.

I am not sure yet what will happen to him, whether he will stay in jail or be let out again. I don't know what will happen if he tries to come after me. I am afraid of him!"

There was a look of shock on both Ben's and Mama's faces.

"Do James's parents know any of this? Do they know he is in jail? He could be charged with attempted murder!"

"I don't know, Ben. I do know that his two brothers, Nat, and Tom, helped Patrick get James to the Flagstaff Courthouse. I would hope that one of them told their parents, but I do not know if they did. It is not my responsibility, although, of course, the baby I lost would have been their first grandson. They may not even know or care if they have a granddaughter. I thought about going to see them while I am here to introduce them to Emma but considering how badly they treated James when he was growing up, and the fact that James tried to kill me, I see no reason why I should involve them in Emma's life."

"I can certainly understand why you would feel that way," Ben said. "We have not seen or heard from them since the day you and James left. What kind of parents have so little interest in the welfare of one of their children?"

"There is more. One of the ranch hands, Luke, became a good friend to James for a while, but also of mine. Luke was upset to see how James was treating me, and James became dangerously jealous of Luke, and thought he was paying too much attention to me.

James even thought, somehow, that Luke was my baby's father, not him. I can't imagine how he could have thought that. Luke has helped me through some really difficult times with James, but we have never been close, like that. Luke is someone I have come to cherish, but I do not know if I am in love with him." A sob escaped me, and I dabbed my eyes.

"Please understand, I was a devoted wife until James almost killed me. I never crossed him or openly disobeyed him, even when I wanted to. Luke has been nothing but respectful and a good friend. He only shared his feelings with me when I told him I would be returning home to New Hampshire for a while. He was desperate to know if I would be coming back."

Tears were streaming down Mama's face and she fought to regain some composure. "You and James have been married for such a short time. It breaks my heart to hear about this. Do you think there could ever be a way for the two of you to work things out? Perhaps if James were to get some help with his drinking?"

"I do not think James and I can ever reconcile after what he did to me. Quite honestly, I do not think he ever really wanted to be married to me. He certainly never wanted to be a father! And yet, I am legally married to him. I do not know how to proceed. Do I simply continue as I am, a married woman separated from her husband? The only way I could ever remarry is if James and I are divorced. And what would people say about me then?"

I was sobbing now.

"Oh, Sarah, I am so sorry this has happened to

you," said Ben, "but it seems all the blame is on James. We will need to think about this and see what might be best for you and little Emma. I have a friend in Conway who is a lawyer, perhaps he can advise us. I will write to him."

Chapter Forty-One

The next day, after a restless sleep, I asked Ben if we could borrow the wagon and a horse so we could go visit Jacob and his family for a few days. I really needed a respite from the stress of my situation, and I knew the children would adore the farm and the lake.

I knew my way by heart, of course, and not much had changed since I was last here. The road in was still a long, bumpy two-lane dirt track through the woods, but at the end the vista opened to my favorite image: the log cabin my father had built, and where I was born, the barn and the lake beyond surrounded by cliffs and mountains. My heart sang! Now this feels like home.

Luna jumped down right away with joyful barks when we arrived, and I could hear answering barks from another dog. Soon we were enveloped by Jacob, Alice and Skye, a beautiful Border Collie from the Benson farm. Skye and Luna greeted each other and decided all was well. Charlie, an unsteady toddler, and the infant, Billy joined us. Jacob offered to give me a tour. Julia and Emma went off to explore with the dogs.

Everything was almost as I had remembered it.

I was impressed by how much more woodland had been cleared for haying and grazing. A huge vegetable garden was just finishing its work for the season, with a few pumpkins, winter squash and beans still waiting to be harvested. There was an area beyond the garden where Jacob had planted fruit trees, that were just beginning to ripen apples and pears. And, of course, there was the chicken coop which I remembered well and Mama's story of the night the fox got into it.

I am a little girl again. Jacob and I are chasing each other between the rows of corn and laughing. Sunny is barking to share our joy. Then the storm clouds came and later the rain. the thunder, the lightening, the terrible wind! Oh, the storm! How scary it is! I can hear the trees cracking and falling to the ground with a crash. I shake my head to clear the memory.

I have always been most taken by the view of the lake. How I had missed it. In the late afternoon sun, the mountains stood proudly in silhouette to the sun slowly setting behind them. Yellow, pink, and orange clouds gave way to purple and gray. In all my life, I will never lose sight of that view. Is this where I am meant to be?

"Our Papa would have been so proud of what you have done here," I said, my voice cracking. "I am too! This is what he dreamed of. You and Alice have been able to expand his dream, our parents' dream, for this place! You have brought Papa alive for me again."

Jacob put his arm around my shoulders, and we stood quietly for a moment.

"I often wish he were here to see what I have

done," Jacob said softly. "And to see you, as well, all grown up, an accomplished and beautiful woman! I know you probably do not remember him, but I do. I miss him every day. I often feel him here with me, watching over my family." Oh, Jacob, I miss him too– the idea of him. And the happy parts of our childhood. Is he here with you? If I stay here, will I find him again? Do I need to find him again?

Julia offered to help Alice prepare dinner for all of us and Emma 'helped' too, so I could spend some more time talking with Jacob. I shared a little of what I had told Mama and Ben, and my dilemma about filing for divorce from James.

"I am so sorry this has happened though from what you told me when I visited it seemed like a possible outcome. I am proud of you for standing your ground in this sad matter. May I come with you when you return to town so we can talk with Mama and Ben before you see the lawyer?"

"I would like that, Jacob. Your support means so much to me!"

Dinner was delicious. Alice had made a special spread for us with fresh trout that Jacob had caught from the lake earlier in the day. She had pan fried them with butter and onions and seasoned breadcrumbs. A variety of fresh vegetables and fruit from the garden completed our meal. Emma had never eaten fish before and was not sure about it but was willing to take a bite. She loved it! A lovely feeling of peace came over me as we sat by candle-light and watched the light outside fade away.

I had forgotten the sleeping porch that Ben had added when his children were small. It was chilly, but with lots of quilts it was perfect for Emma, Julia, Luna, and me. It brought back fond memories of hearing the wind moving through the pine trees and the calling of the loons. Julia and Emma were both startled when the loons began calling as we lay in our beds, but they were not afraid. Every hoot echoed over the lake along with their strange shrieks and "laughter", and later the mournful calls that sent chills up my spine. They would be leaving the lake soon for the winter.

"I wonder what they are saying to each other," Emma said before she drifted off to sleep.

The three of us stayed at the farm for a few days, helping with the chores, the final harvesting of the garden, and keeping the boys entertained so Alice could have a break. Julia was wonderful with Charlie and the baby, and when I mentioned going back into town, she asked if she and Emma could stay a few more days.

"It is like heaven out here," said Julia "It is magical–like nowhere I have ever been before."

"I will be taking Jacob with me into town. I am sure Alice would enjoy your company and help with the little ones. Why don't you go ask her? I will check with Jacob."

The next morning Jacob and I hitched up the horse to the wagon again and headed back into town. It was only a few miles but seemed a world away.

"I understand you are thinking of divorcing James. If you succeed, have you decided what you want to do or where you want to live?" Jacob asked.

"That is part of why I am here," I said. "So many decisions. These past few days at the farm have brought back many happy memories, but also sad ones. You said you feel our father there and I wonder if I would feel his presence as well, if perhaps I built a small house for Emma and me and, of course, Luna, near you. I could help you and Alice with the farm work. I just do not know if that would be enough for me. And would it change things for you and Alice."

"I was impressed, when I visited you in Arizona, how important you had become to the working of the ranch. How you had become part of the ranch 'family'. I can imagine that would be hard to give up."

"Yes," I said softly. "There is also Luke. You met him, I think? He loves me and has become very dear to me as well. If I were free to marry again, I might choose to marry him. And I do love being part of the ranch family, and my close friends Blue and Grace in Flagstaff. "

"I can understand why this is so hard for you," Jacob said.

"One thought I had, now that I know travel from here to Flagstaff and from there back here again is not as difficult as it once was, perhaps I do not have to make a choice that can't be undone."

"That is certainly a possibility," said Jake.

Why didn't I think of that before? I love that idea! My spirits rose. I could easily decide to travel home from Arizona to visit, and by the same token, my family could travel there! What a lovely thought!

Chapter Forty-Two

When Jake and I returned to my parent's house in the village, a letter was waiting for me. The postmark was Flagstaff AZ.

"Oh, maybe it is from Blue or Cora!" I said happily, but as soon as I saw the handwriting, my heart sank. James. I hesitated to open the envelope and handed it to Jake.

"Jake, can you read this letter for me? I don't think I can handle it."

Jakob took the letter into the parlor where Mama and Ben were having tea, and the four of us listened while he read James's letter.

My Dearest Sarah,

"I heard from Tom and Nat that you had returned home to New Hampshire. They have been coming to see me every week or two and told me some of what you went through because of me. I feel so very terrible about what I did to you and our baby. I know you may never be able to forgive me. But I want you to know I still love you with all my heart, and Emma too. I want to find some way to make this up to you.

I have been told I may be able to get out of jail in a few months, possibly next July. I would give anything to be able to talk to you and see if you can ever find it in your heart to let me back into your life. My time in jail has sobered me up properly, and I have promised the judge never to touch another drop of alcohol once I am out on my own, or I will end up back in the slammer.

I miss you and Emma something fierce. Please tell me you may be coming back to Arizona or if I can come see you in New Hampshire when I get out.

Your loving husband,
James Parker

A look of shock passed over everyone's face and I burst into tears.

"The bloody nerve!" said Ben. Yes, the bloody nerve! And what if he decides to come here or seek me out at the ranch when I go back? What if he goes after Luke? I was beside myself!

"Hold on," Jacob said, always the voice of reason. "Sarah does not need to respond to this letter, nor any of us, either. We will be seeing your lawyer friend soon and he can write a letter to James making it clear that Sarah is in no way his dear wife and that she is filing for divorce. We can also file a notice forbidding him to come near her on pain of being returned to jail. Then we should get the papers signed and filed right away in case he thinks he can come after her."

Divorce. How has it all come to this? We loved each other once and set off bravely together into the unknown. Perhaps that was just my dream. I am not sad anymore–I am just angry! Divorce is the answer.

In the end, just Ben and I took the carriage up to Conway to see Mr. Elijah Sullivan, Atty. At Law. His offices were on the ground floor of a home that was much like my parents' but on a smaller scale. It was set on a pleasant tree-lined street off the main thoroughfare in Conway.

Ben had already described my predicament in his letter to his friend, and now presented him with James's letter.

"My, my," Mr. Sullivan said, after reading the letter. "Mr. Parker is not going to give up easily, I see. However, after I send out the divorce papers and the formal restraining order to keep him away from you and your daughter, he will have no option other than to return to jail if he violates the terms of these injunctions. We will file these papers with the court in Flagstaff as well as deliver them to him. Is there anyone else who should receive copies?

"Yes," I said. "His former employer, Patrick McBride of the Copper Stallion Ranch, Flagstaff, Arizona, in case James comes back to him looking for work or retribution."

"Very good. You should have no difficulties after these papers are properly filed. My advice to you, young lady," with a nod to me, "is to stay with your parents for a few months and not return to Flagstaff until at least June. Just be aware, if he is released from jail in the spring, as his letter indicates he might be, you will need to be careful."

While his secretary typed up these documents so that I could sign them, Mr. Sullivan asked me questions about the ranch and my life there. After I signed all the necessary papers and Mr. Sullivan promised me to get all the copies sent in the next days' mail, I felt a huge weight lift off my shoulders.

In a week, maybe a few days more, I will be FREE! I can hardly believe it. I certainly never asked for this to happen, but it did, and now I can be just me. Me and Emma! Of course, it occurred to me that Emma would be growing up without her father, just as I had. But this was different. In this case, I had to protect Emma from her father, not try to keep them connected. We could make a new plan. I can make better choices and Emma and I can be free.

I decided to write a letter to Luke, another to Blue and one to Patrick and Cora. Anything, now, is possible!

Chapter Forty-Three

What a long winter that was staying mostly in town with my family. At first, I did not think there would be anything for me to do, and I could not stand having no chores or some useful tasks to take up my time. Emma was with me, but Julia stayed out at the farm as much as she could. She was uncomfortable in our big house with all its modern conveniences and hired help, and Jacob's family really enjoyed having her with them. Luna was happy to stay at the farm, as well, where she could run free. We also discovered she loved to swim in the lake and did so until it got too cold. I promised Julia we would return to the ranch as early in the spring as we could travel safely.

Emma had a wonderful time with the children, especially Maggie who, at eight, was closest to her in age. I could often hear laughter coming from the playroom and was happy she had other children to play with.

My favorite part of the time I spent in that big house was the time I spent with Mama in her sewing room. I told her I had been longing to relearn how to sew and she was delighted to show me how on her second sewing machine, the one that Sallie Mae used when they worked together on a project. Maggie was also learning to sew and had already started working on her first "big" quilt. Sometimes Maggie and Emma watched my lessons, and sometimes Emma and I watched Maggie as she carefully traced shapes on pieces of fabric and cut them out with scissors almost too big for her to hold. With enormous concentration, she sewed each piece together and then pieced them into her "blanket", as she liked to call it. I was impressed by how well she paid attention to every detail and how careful she was using the sewing machine, especially since she could just barely reach the treadle.

Mama was pleased when Emma showed an interest in learning how to sew. At almost three she was too young to use the sewing machine, but she liked making the machine "go" by pushing up and down on the treadle underneath. When it was my turn to sew, Maggie showed Emma how to carefully draw lines on a piece of fabric and then cut out the shape, although Emma did not yet have the dexterity to do that. I think Mama was totally in her element as she showed us how to make quilts. Much laughter came from our little sewing bee.

Until the snow came, I took Emma in the wagon out to the farm two or three days per week to visit for a day, and sometimes I took the other children as well, with all of us well bundled up against the cold. Luna and Skye always greeted us with shrieking barks of happiness, wagging their entire bodies in joy. I missed Luna so much, but this was a better place for her than in town.

Since there had not been much snow yet, we

tested the ice on the lake and found it strong enough to skate on, at least around the edges. How exciting, such a rare event. Everyone had skates except Julia, (mine were quite old but serviceable) and we found an extra pair that fit Julia. What an adventure–skating on the pond overlooked by the cabin, surrounded by cliffs and mountains and woods. It was a once in a lifetime treat. Julia was excited and awestruck by this opportunity.

Meanwhile, Julia had been secretly writing in her journal about her trip, as her mother had suggested. (She shared some of her entries with me, but no one else.) She added notes almost every day about what she had seen and experienced, both at the farm and in town. Of course, there were lots of entries about her journey by train as well. She also added photos that Becky had taken of everyone playing in the snow or skating on the lake or just posing on the Verandah so Julia would be able to take everyone "home" with her. It was a wonderful project and she seemed to be totally invested in it.

It was now well into November. I had received wonderful letters from Blue and from Cora congratulating me on the news of my impending divorce and looking forward to my return. I had not told them about my letter from James. I began to worry that I had not heard back from Luke, but he did finally write to me.

Dear Sarah,

I hope you and Emma are well. It feels like you are both so far away from me. This place is not the same without you.

I was happy to get your recent letter, and to hear you have filed for divorce. I am looking forward to the time you will return, and we can talk about what may come next.

I do need to tell you that Tom and Nat have been visiting James often. They are both upset about what James did to you, but they are also feeling torn, since he is their brother.

Nat told me that James had received the papers your lawyer sent with a copy of a divorce decree and a letter saying he could not come near you or little Emma or he will go back to jail. James is furious I can tell you. This is some ugly business. Who knows what he may try to do when he gets out of jail? I guess we will have some things to sort out, somehow, when you come back.

I hope those papers from your lawyer that you signed really stick!

Your true friend, Luke

Chapter Forty-Four

Thanksgiving and Christmas came and went with great festivities, wonderful food, and merriment. Not to mention dozens of presents for everyone. Jacob brought his family and Julia into town on his sleigh, and we all shared rooms with one another for several days of family togetherness. It was quite lovely, but I was overwhelmed by so many people in one place! I was glad when we could return to the relative peace and quiet of every-day life.

In January we had a major snowstorm, which brought life in our village to a standstill for several days. That did not stop the children from going out to make snow forts and to try out their new sleds on a small nearby hill. We were also able to set out on skis or snowshoes to explore this wonderland.

There was great excitement leading up to Emma's third birthday and much secrecy as my siblings plotted and planned the perfect celebration and gifts for their little niece. The 21st promised to be a dazzlingly bright day, very cold and not a cloud in the sky. Everything sparkled as the sun bounced off the snow crystals.

Sallie Mae made a special lunch at Becky's request, but dinner was even more special. All of Emma's favorite dishes followed by a magnificent chocolate cake decorated with three candles and an extra candle "to grow on".

Each of the girls had made something for Emma, Lyddie a watercolor painting of the lake, Maggie a small doll's quilt for her new doll, a set of photos taken by Becky when they were all at play outside so Emma could remember them when she returned to Arizona in the spring. Benny worked with Ben to make a wooden doll bed just the right size for Blue. Mama made Emma her very own quilt (which she somehow kept a secret during our lessons). Gladys and Sallie Mae made little cakes and candies to share, all wrapped up with fancy ribbon as well as making the table settings for both lunch and dinner extra fancy. Emma glowed with all the attention and the gifts! We missed having Jacob and his family and Julia there, but the next time they were able to get into town on their sleigh they arrived with several small gifts for Emma, which gave her a second "mini-birthday".

There seemed to me to be a great difference in the snowstorms here from the storms I experienced at the ranch. It came to me finally that it was the piercing winds of the open fields that were missing and the dryness of the desert air. Here we were protected by towering trees, and nearby hills and mountains, and the snow was sometimes wet and heavy. There the open landscape seemed to go on for miles before the mountains finally rose as a barrier. I could not say one was any better than the other-both were cold!

By March, the snows had mostly ended and soon

the mud began. Days of rain made it impossible to go out on foot where there were no wooden walkways and traveling by wagon or carriage became almost impossible. Finally, after the rains stopped and the earth began to dry out, Jacob was able to bring Alice, Julia, and the boys to visit us, along with Luna. It had been only a few months but seemed like forever that we had all been together. What a fun time we had! The weather had become much warmer, and the children could play outside, a wonderful change from being cooped up inside during mud season.

All during these months, even while distracted with learning to sew or going on outdoor adventures with Emma and the other children, I never lost sight of my true purpose in being "at home." It had become clear to me that I must return to Arizona. Even though my roots were with my family here, my future lay at the ranch. There I had become somebody, a cherished friend with an important role to play.

I was grateful, however, that, except in the quiet moments before I fell asleep, I could be distracted from my constant thoughts of Luke and James and what I might face me when I returned in a few short months.

Chapter Forty-Five

I became nervous as June approached. I had heard nothing further from James, which was a relief, and I was encouraged by letters from Cora and Patrick, and from Blue and Grace that my return was eagerly anticipated. Luke had written several times. He was eager to see me as well but also nervous about what James might do when he was released. I had heard nothing yet about when his sentence might be lifted. I contacted our lawyer in Conway, NH, and he had heard nothing as well. His advice was to "keep my head down and don't go looking for trouble"!

In mid-June I visited Jacob and Alice with our wagon for the last time. Jacob and I took a long walk together and I marveled once again how close we still were after all these years and how easily we could talk about anything. He promised that he would come visit again and bring Mama and Ben with him if he could persuade them. He also promised he would write and keep me up to date on the family. Julia told me how much she loved this place on the lake but that she was also ready to go home. Alice was sad to lose her friend and helper but understood her need to go home to her own family. I helped Julia pack and returned to town with her and Luna.

A few days later, with Emma and me all packed up for our journey, we said out good-byes. Thankfully, Gladys had carefully packed Emma's new quilt, the doll bed and little quilt, the beautiful quilt Mama made for me and some other treasures we had acquired on this trip, into a large box so we would have less to carry. This box would be shipped right through to Flagstaff. I would have to remember that for next time I traveled east! Emma, however, insisted she wanted to hold onto her doll Blue and promised to be especially careful not to lose or hurt her.

Ben had generously paid our expenses home with additional spending money for anything we might need along the way. An early birthday gift, he said. He had tried to persuade me to stay until my actual birthdate, but I was eager to be on my way. Gladys had put together a lovely basket of sandwiches, fruit, and cookies, as well as food for Luna and jars of water. I feel so well cared for and so loved! My heart is full.

Part V

Spring 1902 – Spring 1903

Chapter Forty-Six

Once again, we were waiting at the train station, surrounded by my family. But this time it was not with bitterness or fear. This time I was filled to overflowing with love and knew I would be coming back. I was also eagerly looking forward to being 'home' again and seeing my friends. Ben and Mama promised to visit us, possibly next spring.

Of course, there were tears, many tears, but they were not for despair, knowing our parting was not permanent. What a difference from only a few years ago when James and I defied our parents and left, with no thoughts of ever returning!

I debated whether to send a telegram with details of our arrival and decided, except for telling Blue, I wanted this to be a surprise. She alone would meet us, and then come with us out to the ranch. I could not wait to see the looks on everyone's face when we showed up unannounced. I was also pleased that Blue would finally meet my ranch "family". I am nervous about meeting Luke again. Having Blue with me may give me courage and make that meeting less stressful. Luke and I will have plenty of time to talk and get comfortable with each other later.

This trip west was much easier than my previous two trips. Julia and Emma were entranced by the passing scenery and entertained each other telling stories about what they saw. "Blue" joined in the fun by waving out the window. Emma told us "Blue" was excited to be on this trip. Emma was more grown up this time and did not fuss at all except for the few occasions when she became over tired. Julia was excited to see her mother and brothers and sister again and did not pester me with hundreds of questions like last time. I was able to relax and read a bit. Even Luna, although I am sure she was sorry to leave the farm, seemed more relaxed. I was sure that once she saw the ranch, she would be back to her joyful self again in no time.

My heart began pounding as the train approached Flagstaff. I started gathering up our belongings, trying to calm myself by keeping busy. Luna picked up my energy and began turning in circles and whining a little. I assured her we were almost home. I swear she understands everything I say.

"Sarah," Julia said, taking hold of my sleeve. "Are you OK? You are shaking."

I laughed. "I am fine. Just feeling a bit nervous. We're almost at the end of our journey. Emma, look around you and make sure you have everything that is yours."

I kept straining my gaze out ahead, trying to catch the first glimpse of the station. Julia, Emma and "Blue" did the same. At last, the sound of the wheels changed as the train began to slow, then there was a loud blast of the horn, and there it was. And there was Blue, standing in the middle of the platform., her arms outstretched with Grace beside her. Oh, how I have missed you, both!!

Once we were safely off the train and our bags handed down, I ran towards Blue, and Grace and we met in a warm embrace.

'Welcome home," Blue said. "I have missed you! I have been waiting impatiently for this moment!"

"And I you, my friend," I said, kissing her on the cheek. Emma ran to us then, and Blue hugged her and tried to pick her up. "Oh my, child, you have grown so big since I last saw you! I have missed you and your mama from the moment you left last fall!"

Grace embraced me and then Emma in a big hug. "What a big girl you are!" she exclaimed.

"Look, Miss Blue, I have a new doll and I named her after you!"

Blue and I laughed in appreciation. "How sweet," Blue said. "She is lovely. Was she a gift from your family?"

"Two of Mama's sisters gave her to me at Christmas."

"She will not let go of this doll for anything," I said. "Blue' chattered throughout this journey just like Emma did. It made me happy to know that she had a friend like I do."

Blue greeted Julia and Luna. As usual, Luna was full of joy. Julia had never met Grace or Blue until now.

"I have heard so much about you and your beautiful shop," said Julia. "It is a pleasure to finally meet you." She gave them each a little curtsey. Her mother has taught her well.

After securing the box packed with our treasures and our baggage, we loaded up the wagon Blue had borrowed for our trip out to the ranch and stopped by the shop to let Grace off so she could tend the shop.

"I am so looking forward to a long visit with you and Emma when you can find the time. We have missed you sorely over this long winter," Grace said. I promised to come as soon as I was settled and could spend a day off the ranch.

Chapter Forty-Seven

I was all nerves and butterflies on our way to the ranch, but at least I had the distraction of Emma and Julia asking Blue lots of questions about what had happened in these parts while we were gone. Thankfully, Blue happily accommodated them. As the road opened into the open fields, Blue and I both gasped at the springtime beauty all around us. The grass was not yet tall but was a vibrant green and wildflowers were just coming into bloom. It was breathtaking.

"I am beginning to understand your love of this area," said Blue. "It is truly lovely!" Then she lowered her voice to a whisper, "There are things you need to know before we get to the ranch.".

Blue and I were sitting up front while Luna and the girls were in the back. I asked them to be quiet for a little while so we could talk.

"I do not know much—you will need to learn the rest from James's brothers. But I did hear James has been released and might be heading out to California with his gambling buddies. Of course, he has no idea you have come home, since you wanted to keep it a surprise. I think that was smart on your part. But I don't think it will be a surprise for long. James and his brothers are pretty tight. They were visiting him every week or two when he was in jail. I do not know where he is now. Be careful."

When we came to the spot where James had kicked me off the wagon, I flinched and began to cry.

"Sarah, what is it? Is this the place?" I nodded 'yes'. And she put her arm around me.

"It will never happen again! Everyone on the ranch will protect you, though possibly not James's brothers. And I know, from what you have told me, Luke will never let any harm come to you. As always, I will welcome your visits to me and Grace in Flagstaff anytime you like.

"I am so lucky to have you in my life," I said, drying my tears. "It seems strange in a way, but my friendship with you is more important to me that the loving bonds I have with my blood-family. You and Patrick and Cora and Luke are my family now. And Grace, of course. I do not know how I could live without any of you."

Soon, the sight of the house and barn came into view. Immediately, Luna bolted from the wagon and made a beeline towards the barn, barking frantically all the way. There were answering barks from the barn. I laughed and cried as I saw first one person and then several appear in the barn door and then in the clearing by the house. Then they were running towards us, waving their hats, and cheering, all of them. My heart leapt at the sight. I am overcome! These are MY people. I love them all!

Patrick and Cora reached us first.

"Welcome, welcome, dearest friend! You have returned! Thank heaven you are here again!"

We descended from the wagon and Patrick gave me a bear hug and Cora kissed my cheek I noticed that her belly was considerably rounder than I remembered it, and Cora winked at me when she saw me notice. They each welcomed Julia with more hugs and kisses. Then I introduced my good friend Blue. They made much of Emma.

"My goodness," Cora said, giving Emma a warm hug. "You have grown up into a beautiful little girl in just a few months!

"Why did you not tell us you were coming so we can give you a proper welcome?" said Patrick.

"I wanted it to be a surprise and I guess I succeeded! There is plenty of time for celebration after we are rested from our long journey," I said. "Right now, I want to greet all my friends here and introduce Blue to everyone, and Emma will need to be put to bed soon, after we eat something."

Soon we had a small crowd surrounding us and I noticed Luke off to the side, looking nervous. Our eyes met, and I smiled. He nodded and returned my smile with warmth. How handsome you are! I have missed you so much!

Then I saw Tom and Nat near the back of the group, their eyes on me. I could not read their expressions, but they took their hats off in greeting when our eyes met. I raised my hand in return. I knew I should go talk to them, but I felt uncomfortable. Who knows what they are thinking? I decided it would be better to talk to them away from everyone.

When I could break away from the hugs and greetings I walked towards Luke. The awkwardness between us was palpable.

"I am happy to see you, Luke," I began, clumsily. He reached for my hand. I could feel him tremble.

"I missed you. What a surprise! I am happy to see you too." He stumbled a little over the words.

"Oh, Luke. It has been so long! Let's find time tomorrow to talk and catch up away from everyone. Tonight, I am exhausted and overcome by this lovely homecoming. Emma needs to be fed and put to bed and I need to rest before I collapse."

"Yes. There is much for us to talk about. I am glad you are finally home again." He squeezed my hand. Out of the corner of my eye, I saw Tom and Nat watching us, and I stepped away.

"Be careful," I whispered. "Nat and Tom are right over there. It won't be long before James knows I have returned, and that they saw us together. I haven't spoken to them yet, and I need to find out how things stand with them and me and where James is. Blue told me he has been released from jail, but she has no idea where he is. I also need to get my bearings now that I am home again." Home again! There, I have said it.

"We'll talk tomorrow".

I left him to collect Emma from Julia and Cora. Emma was having a grand time with everyone commenting on how grown up she was and how pretty, but I could also see she was near her limit. There would be a meltdown soon if I did not intervene. I also wanted to speak with Blue before she left. She was talking with Ricardo, a new hand who had been hired to take James's place. I took Emma over to them, and when it came time for Blue to leave, he offered to accompany her on horseback to be sure she returned to Flagstaff safely. We both thanked him for his kind offer, and I embraced Blue before she mounted the wagon.

"I will call on you very soon," I promised. "Thank you for helping me orchestrate this wonderful day!"

This homecoming felt surreal to me, the greetings, hugging, welcome speeches. I had not even been up to my little cabin yet, and I needed some time there to gather myself together. Emma too. We needed to be home together. Plenty of time the next day and forever after to figure everything out.

The old photographer's words came back to me: 'Someday I will arrive at the place where I belong, and I will know I am home!'

Chapter Forty-Eight

Being in my own space again with Emma felt so right. She seemed happy to be home and fell asleep as soon as I got her fed and settled. I lay in my bed and just stared at the ceiling until I, too, finally succumbed to exhaustion, dreaming of strong arms around me and hot kisses.

The next morning, I was up early, my body throbbing with new energy. Luna apparently felt the same and went bolting out into the new day with extra enthusiasm. I immediately set about unpacking my belongings and Emma's from our journey. The big box with all its treasures was still down by the barn and I knew it could wait, but I wanted to get everything stowed and the bedding washed and replaced in anticipation of what the evening might hold. I also sorely needed washing myself and Emma too. Too bad, no hot and cold running water here or a lovely big tub to soak in. Oh well, there are more important things in life!

Emma was quite the chatterbox all morning, retelling her stories of our joyful homecoming and remembering happy events from our trip. She continued to carry 'Blue' with her, and 'Blue' made some remarks about the journey as well, especially about the fun she had on the train.

I asked Emma, once, if she missed her papa. In all seriousness, she answered: "Papa is not nice." I gave her a hug and told her I felt the same. "It is not likely we will see Papa for a long time."

In late afternoon, Luke appeared, hat in hand. He was dressed in fresh clothes and his hair was still damp from washing. My heart is pounding. I have not felt like this for far too long.

"I hope you had a restful night," Luke said awkwardly. "How are you and Emma doing after your long journey?"

"We both had a good night, thank you for asking. We have been making our little cabin ship shape after being away for so long."

"Do you have time to go walking? We can take Emma, of course, and Luna" Luke said.

"That would be nice," I responded. "We could have dinner together later, if you like."

We set off through the grass, just starting to grow. Luna ran happily ahead, and Emma toddled along with us, trying but failing to keep up with Luna. Luke took my hand and we walked quietly together. How peaceful, how lovely. No drama. No demands

We turned to each other after walking for a while and Luke put his arms around me.

"I want to be with you," Luke whispered into my ear.

"I want to be with you too," I whispered back. "But there is also something I need to tell you. It does not change anything about how I feel about you, but I need you to know."

"What is it?"

"I do not know yet if I can marry again."

I felt Luke stiffen in my arms.

"Please Luke—please understand. My marriage was a disaster. I do not want to ever repeat what I went through as a married woman. I know you well enough to know you would never do anything to hurt me. It is not that." I paused, trying to find the words. "I am actually not sure what is holding me back. I just feel like I need to keep my independence. At least for a while longer."

"Yes, I understand. But I want so much for us to be a family, to have a child together! I do not want you to feel as if I own you. I want you to feel as independent as you wish to be. Let's talk about it."

"Oh, Luke, you are everything I could ask for in a husband and father for Emma, and for our children in the future. I just need a little more time to get used to the idea."

We walked together and talked for some time until we were back at the cabin and Emma needed to be fed and put into her bed. We had settled nothing except that we loved each other and wanted to be together. We held each other for a long time, and he kissed me gently before he returned to the barn for the night. I did not want to let him go.

The next day I began preparing for laying out the new garden, checking on our seed supply and planning what I wanted to plant. I checked the garden plot and could see we would need a lot of digging and prep work. Emma came with me to check out the condition of the garden, and, of course, Luna, as well. We had a busy day, but I could not erase the images and sensations of the previous night. I was overtaken by my thoughts.

In the early evening, Luke reappeared, hat in hand. He smelled of soap and cleaned clothes and was as handsome as I had ever seen him. Inside the door of my cabin, he pulled me close.

"Last night I did not want to leave you," he whispered. "I promise you I will never push you any faster than you are willing or able to go, but I WILL marry you one day! I promise you that too!"

"I know you have waited a long time for us to be together. I have too. It has been a long time since I have been with... someone. I think if anyone could persuade me, it would be you. But my feelings are still tender. Thank you for your understanding!"

He kissed me then, soft, and sweet. "We will talk more about this next time. We just need to get used to each other."

"Yes," I said.

He winked, tipped his hat to me with a smile and was gone. I slept alone, dreaming happy dreams. I remembered a snippet of one dream in which I was standing on top of a hill, wearing a white dress, and carrying a basket of flowers. I woke up smiling, greeting a beautiful, balmy day. The sun was getting brighter and there was a soft breeze. My favorite kind of day.

"Come, Emma," I said. "Let's make breakfast." I helped her get dressed and wash her face and hands. Together we made oatmeal with a few nuts and berries mixed in and a dollop of applesauce. It was a lovely breakfast.

"Emma, I want to talk to you about Luke and your papa. You know Luke is a good friend. I care a lot about him. Now that you and I are back home from visiting your Grandma Hannah and Grandpa Ben, Luke and I want to spend time together, to make up for some of the time we missed. Do you understand?"

"yes, I think so," said Emma.

"Your Papa is no longer part of our family. Do you remember, we talked about that? Papa and I are no longer married to each other. He is far away and likely will not be coming back." I crossed my fingers behind my back. "I remember you saying you did not think he was a nice man."

"Papa scares me sometimes."

"How do you feel about Luke?"

"He is nice. He gives me hugs."

"Here is a hard question for you. I will explain the best I can. What if Mama and Luke became such good friends, they wanted to be together all the time, except, of course, when Luke or Mama is working? You know how Luke works with the cattle and is gone during the day and I work with the chickens and in the garden. When Luke is finished working in the evening, he would come back to our cabin. The three of us would eat dinner together, and he would visit with me for a while after you go to sleep and then go back to the barn where he lives. How would you feel about that?"

"I think that would be alright." She hesitated. "But will you still love me just the same?"

"Oh, dearest one, of course I will! Luke loves you too. So now you will have Mama and Luke and Luna, all loving you." I gave her a big hug and nuzzled her in the neck until she giggled. "So, what do you think about that, baby girl?"

Still laughing, Emma said, "I think I like it!"

Oh, this is so much harder than I thought it would be! How can a little child, not even four years old, understand how the grown-ups in her life feel about each other? I guess this will be a work in progress! At least Luna likes Luke and is not surprised by his visits.

Luke and I fell into a rhythm that felt right to each of us. We talked for a while before and during dinner, including Emma in our conversations. He returned to the barn (not happily), after we had spent some time talking more privately.

Luke is all I could ask for in a father for my

beloved Emma, and I DO love him. He is nothing like James. I could never be afraid of him. What is stopping me from agreeing to be married? Do I just need more time or is there something else? These thoughts would not leave me be, but I was beginning to soften to the idea of marrying Luke.

Chapter Forty-Nine

I began my work in the garden in earnest. Julia joined me in planting everything we could think of, since not all crops last through the hot summer months in this climate. We put up pole "tepees" for climbing beans, cucumbers, and other vining crops. I had brought some sweet corn seeds from home to try and planted them in "hills", the way I had been taught by my mama as a child. Tomatoes of several varieties went in with supports made of wood, sweet peppers, and, of course, greens of various types where there was partial shade during the day. Summer and winter squash, yellow bush beans (my favorite) and, of course, several varieties of sunflowers for both chickens and human consumption.

It was interesting and fun to try different types and varieties of vegetables and fruits each new season, to see what might grow and even thrive in this soil and climate. What I loved most about this part of my responsibilities was having free reign over every aspect of the garden. I loved my independence and being able to make my own decisions.

This season, with no rain in sight, we worked

hard to bring some water down from the stream for the new plantings and prayed for the monsoon rains which usually came later in the summer. There was little water in the 'tank' we had built.

I visited with Cora several days each week to catch up with her family and to see how she was doing with her pregnancy. Emma came with me and enjoyed seeing Julia and her little sister, Katie. Julia had told me her mother seemed more tired that she had been with her previous pregnancies but was otherwise fine.

One day I found Cora relaxing on a chaise-longue on the verandah in the shade, with a fan swinging over her from the ceiling. She was not asleep, however.

"How nice to see you, Sarah," she said, as I approached. "I think it will only be a few more weeks. Can I count on you to help me birth this child?"

"Of course, Cora. You can count on me if Julia can assist. She did a wonderful job when it was my time."

"I remember. Julia is a clever girl and will be indispensable. But I want you to help me birth this child."

"I will be happy to. Just let me know how you are doing and when you may need me. Also, be sure to tell Julia what you need her to prepare, so you will be ready for me."

"Of course. Thank you so much, Sarah. I feel happy, knowing you will be with me. I think it will be an easy birth. I am pretty experienced, after all." She laughed. "Nothing for you to worry about!"

Oh my, soon it will be my turn to help another woman bring a new life into this world!

As the summer progressed, so did my relationship with Luke. Emma matured as well, and I could see her becoming more and more attached to Luke, which made me (and him) feel happy. Luke and I had talked about becoming "engaged", which could be made public, any time we wished it to be broadcast. I was not quite ready. However, I was getting there.

How strange it feels, to love someone but not be ready to publicly acknowledge him. What does that mean? I know Luke feels hurt by this. Luke, I am sorry. My heart still feels so raw. I just can't open myself to such hurt again! How can I get past this?

In early August, I visited Cora again. Her belly was enormous and looked like it could explode at any minute.

"It won't be long, now, Sarah. Julia will have everything ready: clean sheets, sterilized scissors and the necessary clean cloths, blankets, and nappies. All you need to do is show up ready and willing to catch the baby. This will be my fifth, after all. What can go wrong? I will ring the cowbell when the time comes and Paddy will come for you as well, day or night."

"I have to admit, Cora, I am a little nervous! You will talk me through it, will you? And I know Julia will be a great help. And what about Emma? I can't leave her alone."

"You will do fine, my friend. Don't you worry none. You will know what to do. And bring Emma with you–she can play with Katie and the boys will be home to watch her."

I busied myself in the garden, which was growing well, now that the rains had finally arrived, and playing with Emma. I needed something to take my mind off what was to come. Cora had loaned me a few books that would be suitable to read to Emma, and we spent part of each day reading and talking about the pictures and the story in the book we were reading. Emma loved it. My evenings and nights with Luke continued to be blissful, but I began to think we needed more space in our small cabin, now that Emma was growing older. I began planning what adding another room might look like and determined to talk to Luke when he returned for dinner.

My daydreaming was interrupted by the distant clanging of a cowbell and then Paddy in the doorway calling my name. He was out of breath.

"It's Mama–the baby is coming. Come quick!"

I grabbed my clean apron. "Emma–it is time to go visit Miss Cora and Katie for a while. You can bring 'Blue' with you. Come quick, now." I picked her up since walking with her down to the house might take some time.

When I reached the house, Patrick greeted me with a big grin on his face.

"It's her time, alright! Soon we will have another wee babe in the house. Here, lass," he said, holding out his arms for Emma. "Let's go join the others and play while your mama is busy."

Julia appeared and led me into Cora's bedroom, which I had not been in before. Two large windows let in plenty of light. Cora was lying on her bed on a clean sheet, with extra pillows behind her. She was flushed and panting, but she gave me a weak smile as I approached.

"In the kitchen," she said, breathily, "there is hot water and cloths. You can wash your hands in there. Hurry!" I returned as quickly as I could, with extra cloths to arrange under her hips. Cora groaned, then let out a cry as I gently moved her legs apart and placed them into position. Julia helped to hold Cora's knees while she spoke to her with words of encouragement. Cora panted hard, then cried out again.

Julia said softly to me, "Mama has been like this for a while, panting and crying with every pain, but her labor has not progressed at all. It is not like her other births."

I nodded and said to Cora, "Don't push, yet. Keep breathing and panting and with the next contraction you can push then." Another wave of pain came over Cora and this time she screamed.

"I think there's something wrong, "she said, huskily. "This birth should be easy. Something does not feel right."

I put my hands on her swollen belly and tried to feel the baby. Julia did as well, and we looked at each other without saying anything.

"Cora, I think your baby is not positioned properly. It is either sideways or possibly coming feet first. What do I do?"

"Push your sleeves up as far as they will go," she said weakly. Another contraction made her cry out again. When she could speak, she said, "put the fingers of your right hand together in a point. You will need to insert your fingers and your whole hand inside me and continue until you can feel the baby." She was panting hard, tears rolling down her face. Julia wiped her face with a damp cloth.

With my heart in my mouth, I did as she instructed until I felt the infant's foot. "Cora, I have the baby's foot!" I began rotating the infant as gently as I could to the left, like the hands of a clock, a little at a time, while Cora continued to scream. By this time Patrick had come into the room, wondering what on earth was going on.

"It's the baby, Patrick. It is trying to come feet first," I said. Sweat was rolling down my face.

Julia, meanwhile, was trying to turn the baby from the outside in the same direction I was, with a gentle massage action with her hands. After a few minutes I felt a tiny bottom and soon a shoulder and finally a head. I gently withdrew my hand and wiped it with one of the cloths.

"We did it, Cora! Julia and I turned your baby! Rest a few minutes, if you can, then we can start pushing again." I was crying with relief. It is not over yet, but hopefully we are over the worst!

Another contraction came. Cora grunted her pain and gave a mighty push. I felt some movement of the infant. Cora was panting hard. Julia held her hand on one side and Patrick on the other.

"Again, Cora, push hard with the next contraction. I think your baby is coming."

With another mighty push and a scream, the head appeared and soon the rest of the tiny body. I caught her as she slithered out in a gush of mucous. A baby girl! I quickly rubbed her with a towel and then wrapped her up in a clean cloth. Just then, the baby's high-pitched yells let everyone know she was alive and not happy about it.

"Cora, a beautiful little girl! You can hold her as soon as we clean her up a little more and cut her cord." Julia brought string and the scissors, and I cut the cord after the string was securely tied. We were both crying but trying hard not to show it. I gave the baby to Julia and she gave her to her mother. Cora opened her night dress and place the infant on her breast. Now everyone was crying.

Patrick gave Cora a hug and kiss on the cheek and caressed the top of the baby's head. "Well done, Lass!" he said.

Cora said, weakly, "We already decided, if it was a girl, we want to name her after you, Sarah. We can't think of anyone we would rather name her for than you." Cora looked at Patrick with affection. "It is up to you, my love, to choose a second name we can call her by."

I did not know how to respond to this and stuttered out, "What an honor. I am blessed!" I burst into tears against Patrick's chest, and he held me in a great bear hug.

Chapter Fifty

Exhausted but exhilarated, I returned to my cabin with Emma after I made sure Cora was cleaned up and comfortable and the baby was settled. I was overcome with emotions-excitement, joy, excruciating embarrassment, relief. I did not know what to think or feel at first. Luke arrived shortly after I did, and I just sobbed in his arms until I began to calm.

"But you said the baby was fine! Why are you crying?"

"These are not tears of sadness, Luke. I am just overcome by what I did today. I may have saved Cora's life, and I brought a beautiful living being into this world. And to top it all off, they named the baby after me!"

"I heard about what happened and what you and Julia accomplished. You should feel enormously proud of yourself, Sarah. What you did was brave and wonderful."

"Thank you, Luke. I do. I am amazed at myself! I am just feeling overwhelmed right now." I began to laugh hysterically. I think I am a little bit off balance. I do not know quite how to feel.

"Come, Sarah. You are over tired and have not eaten anything all day. You need to rest for a little while–I will fix you something to eat."

I did as I was told and laid down on my bed. I was beginning to relax a little. Luke sat beside me on the bed and held my hand. I am so grateful for this man!

"Luke, you know how sometimes one of the mares or cows needs help dropping her foal or calf because it is turned around inside her and she is in distress?"

"Yes–Patrick is usually the one who helps turn the fetus. I have watched him do it. It is a scary and amazing thing to see."

"Well, that is what I did for Cora! I put my whole hand and part of my arm inside her and was able to shift the baby's position. I don't know how I did that–just instinct, I guess. And Julia helped from the outside. We were a team, Luke. But now I don't know how I will ever be able to look Cora in the face again. I am so embarrassed, just thinking about it. And Luke, I will never forget feeling those tiny feet and the baby's little bum before she was born." My words tumbled out almost faster than I could think.

"My goodness, Sarah. Is there anything you cannot do?" A mix of admiration and amusement played on Luke's face.

I did not answer. I was suddenly overcome with

fatigue.

The next morning when I awoke, I discovered Luke had made a breakfast of oatmeal for Emma and me before he left. He is a keeper, for sure! I doubt, in a million years, James would have taken such good care of us.

My energy had returned, as had Emma's and after breakfast we went down to the ranch house to see Cora and the new baby. We found Cora sitting up in bed, nursing little Sarah and looking rested and content.

"Good morning, my dear friend and my sweet Emma. Would you like to meet a new little friend? Your mama helped me yesterday to bring this beautiful baby into the world. I have even named her Sarah, just like your mama."

"Like when I named my new doll Blue, after Mama's friend?"

"Yes, very much like that. Here, come closer. You can see her face and her beautiful green eyes." Emma was entranced, as was I. What a perfect little girl. There was even a hint of red hair beginning to show.

"Cora," I began awkwardly, "what I did to help you yesterday, please do not speak of it. I am sorely embarrassed but happy everything turned out well."

"Nonsense, child. I am so grateful you were here and brave enough to do what needed to be done." She

283

looked at Emma, who was transfixed, looking at the baby. "Julia feels as you do, but without the two of you I might well have died and this wee babe as well. I will be forever grateful to you both!"

"Thank you for saying that." I had to wipe my eyes. "Have you decided on a middle name yet? What you will call her, not to cause confusion between us?" I asked.

"We are thinking 'Rosaleen'. It is a Gaelic name. We will call her 'Rosy'. What do you think?"

"I like it, Cora. It is a lovely name. I have a friend I grew up with who named her youngest Rosalie. Emma, meet your new little friend Rosy."

"She is so small, Mama. Will she grow bigger?"

"Of course, she will! You were just that small when you came to me and look at you now!"

Chapter Fifty-One

The next day I decided it was time to go visit Grace and Blue. I took Emma with me. It was a hot day, and we brought water with us to drink along the way. Emma loved the shop and visiting as much as I did. We were both greeted, as always, with hugs and kisses. While they finished their business with a customer, Emma and I looked at the beautiful dresses and fabrics that were on display.

"They should make dresses for little girls like me, and something for babies, too, like Rosy."

Blue overheard Emma's pronouncement.

"Oh, Blue, forgive us. Emma has such a wonderful imagination, not to mention definite opinions about everything."

"Not at all," said Blue. "I think it is a lovely idea. There have even been a few inquiries recently, for such offerings for toddlers and little girls. Possibly even older girls, as the population of Flagstaff grows. Grace and I have even been thinking about this very thing. I wonder if I could make you a proposal?"

"A proposal? What kind of proposal?"

Blue said, "Quite recently, electricity has become available to both homes and businesses in Flagstaff. Grace and I have decided to make an investment of providing electricity to our shop, and to purchase another sewing machine that would be electrified and therefore run much more quickly and efficiently than our old one. My proposal involves you and my old sewing machine. I was wondering if you would like to have it (no, no, it is a gift) and keep it at your place. As you learn more about sewing and become more proficient, perhaps you could make some of the clothes that babies and small children might like or, more to the point, their mothers might like. What do you think?"

"Oh, my goodness! Really? What a marvelous gift! You are too kind!" I was so astonished that I fell over my words, overwhelmed by her generosity. What an astonishing stroke of luck! My very own sewing machine!

"The next thing to do is to get you involved in the sewing group I have talked of. We meet monthly, and it just so happens that we will meet again in a few days. You are welcome to bring Emma and to stay overnight if you wish. I hope you can make arrangements."

"Oh Blue, I would not miss it for the world. How different my life is now–I do not have to ask permission! I will plan to take the sewing machine home with me as soon as I have a place for it. Bless you, my dearest friend.!"

I returned home that afternoon full of excitement and enthusiasm for a potential new venture and for the prospect of going to my first sewing bee. Emma slept most of the way home. We arrived just as Luke appeared.

"Luke, I have something exciting to tell you! Blue has offered me her old treadle sewing machine as a gift! She has decided to invest in electricity for her shop and plans to purchase a new electrified sewing machine. Can you imagine?"

Luke looked blank for the moment, then rallied. "That sounds wonderful, sweetheart. Let's talk about it later, I am exhausted and need some dinner."

"Of course. It is just I am so excited about this new prospect! I just had to tell you right away."

After a simple meal of egg sand toast, with sauteed potatoes and vegetables, I broached the idea of adding an extra room to our cabin, also Blue's invitation to my very first sewing bee.

"I have been thinking, Luke. I need more space in this tiny cabin. I will need a place for my sewing machine and supplies. I wonder if Patrick would be willing to help us pay for adding another room. And perhaps some of the men could help us build the new addition like they did before."

"We can certainly ask him. What is a sewing bee?"

"It is a group of women who get together for a day of sewing and socializing once a month. Most of the women in this bee are from town but a few come from outlying ranches like I do. The groups are sometimes called quilting bees, but the ladies do all kinds of sewing and handwork. Blue has been holding them at her large home in Flagstaff for the past few years and has been urging me to come since we first met. I have not been free to go until now. It would mean staying overnight at her home so I can return by daylight in the morning. She said I could bring Emma if I want to."

"These are two big things to talk about. Can we do that tomorrow?" he said. "I can see your ideas and your point about needing extra space. I agree with that! I just need to think about how we can make an addition work, financially, not to mention explaining why you need so much extra space as a single woman with a small child!

Before I don't like asking Patrick for money, but I have an idea. Do you remember me telling you that when I started working here, I saved most of my pay? Except for new clothes or boots every couple of years, I have spent almost nothing. I am going to count up what I have and invest in what I hope will become our house, eventually." He winked at me. "Maybe that will convince you to marry me!" I laughed.

"And I do like the idea of you meeting and getting to know other women. I know how much your friendships with Blue and Grace mean to you. Plus, it would give you a nice break from all the work you do around here. I can always have dinner with the men at the ranch house. I have been missing Cora's amazing cooking!" he teased, with a grin. "Let's work on one idea at a time. We can squeeze your new sewing machine in somewhere. Maybe Cora will realize on her own that you need more space with your new sewing venture!"

Would James have ever be so thoughtful and aware of my needs? Would he have ever talked to me like this? Would he have ever been so supportive? Luke is perfect. What is the matter with me?

"Luke. I think there is another, bigger issue for us to talk about tomorrow."

"What now?"

I reached out for him and held him against me.

"I have finally realized something. It has taken a while, but now I know for certain: I don't ever want to live without you, Luke. I am so amazed by you and so happy! I want everyone to know how we feel about each other! I think we should talk about getting engaged!"

Luke held me tight and whispered in my ear. "I have been waiting so long to hear you say that! Yes! Let's tell everyone tomorrow. I mean, let's talk about telling everyone tomorrow."

Chapter Fifty-Two

The next day, after Luke returned from the barn, we approached Patrick and Cora at the ranch house with our questions. Emma tagged along. Cora was sitting in the kitchen with Patrick, nursing little Rosy. She looked tired but content. I gave her a big hug and Emma begged to see the baby. Luke stood with his hat in his hand, trying not to look at Cora.

"Come, sit with us," said Patrick. "I can see you are on an errand." He motioned Luke to a chair that partially blocked his view of the nursing baby. Luke looked relieved. I sat next to Patrick.

"We have come with a question. I will let Sarah tell you about her news, but I will just jump in and ask if you might consider helping Sarah to pay for an addition to her cabin. I have been saving part of my pay every month since I started working here and have a decent nest egg hidden away. I would like to help pay for the addition.

"We also have an announcement. You and Cora will be the first to know."

I saw Patrick's eyebrows rise for an instant and Cora's too.

"I see," said Patrick carefully, ever the diplomat. "And what is Sarah's news that has prompted the idea of expanding her living space?"

"Oh, it is not what you think," I said quickly, blushing. "Do you remember meeting my friend Blue, the dressmaker from Flagstaff? She has offered me a wonderful opportunity. She wants me to have her old sewing machine because she is purchasing an electrified one for her busy shop. And I may be able to help her business grow in future by making clothing and accessories for infants and children for her to sell. I will be able to make a small income as well. I will also be able to make clothing for Emma and your children eventually, if you like." I was so excited that I just babbled on about needing an extra bedroom now that Emma was getting older and needing space to sew. "I promise this will not interfere with my other responsibilities."

I glanced at Patrick and saw he was trying not to smile.

"Well, now," he said. "That all sounds mighty important. And what might your announcement be, Luke? Yours and Sarah's? And does that figure into Sarah's need for more space in her cabin?"

Luke looked nervous, and I blushed.

"Well, sir, you may have noticed that Sarah and I have been spending some time together since she returned home."

"Oh, get on with it," said Cora, chuckling. "Everybody knows."

"Well," I spoke up. "It took me a while to be convinced I could marry again, after all I went through with James, but Luke has been very persuasive. We want to announce our engagement and wanted you both to hear it first."

"Well, by thunder!" said Patrick, clapping Luke on the back and giving me a bear hug. "All I can say is Congratulations and it is about time! Cora, my dear, what do you think about this? Should we be helping these two young people make their home bigger and more suitable for a married couple?"

Cora was smiling broadly but dabbed at her eyes. "I think it a wonderful idea, considering they are both part of our ranch family. Do you have any other important news to share with us?" she said, looking pointedly at me.

Luke and I looked at each other and I blushed again. "Not yet," I said. "All in good time."

"That's good enough for me," said Patrick, giving his knee a good slap. "We can talk about what you have in mind and other details later." Cora, of course, was overcome with emotion over this piece of news. She hugged us both and kissed my cheek. Her face was wet with tears.

"I am so happy for you both. You deserve all the joy you can give each other. What would you both like to do to announce your engagement? And when shall we set a date for the wedding.? We will need to plan a celebration!"

"I would love to have a gathering at the ranch house, or outside if it is still warm enough and have lots of food, music, and maybe dancing." (I looked at Luke and saw him grimace). "Like the celebration we have after the fall cattle run or at Christmas. We have not yet thought about the wedding itself. One step at a time! What do you think, Luke?"

"It sounds wonderful, except the dancing". He looked embarrassed.

"I could show you how if you are willing. It is fun."

"We'll see", he said.

We agreed to hold off our engagement celebration until the annual dinner following the cattle run in a few weeks. Cora offered to help me plan.

When we returned to the cabin for dinner, I made a simple meal of an egg scramble stuffed with cheese and vegetables, but neither of us was hungry. When it was clear that Emma was fast asleep, Luke took my hand and led me to my bed.

"I am so grateful you have finally said yes," Luke whispered. He cupped my face in his hands and kissed me, then my arms were around his neck and I leaned into him.

"Have you ever…?" I whispered.

"No. Will you teach me?"

We took it slow, at first, as we each began to undress the other. Clothes fell to the floor as we looked and touched and kissed until we could wait no longer. We fell into bed together, exploring, tasting, crying in our need for each other. Oh, what sweetness! What joy!

Before dawn, Luke slipped away.

In the morning, I arose and put on my robe, so I could let Luna out and lift Emma from her bed. What a magical night! What sweet memories! I could feel Luke's presence and imagine sitting in bed drinking coffee with him and snuggling with Emma. Is this what a family could look like? This is bliss. I wish this moment could last forever.

That afternoon, Luke and I were drawing out lines in the dirt east of the existing bedroom. I could not help but grin at him and he would wink and grin back,

"Last night was so sweet and so loving," I whispered. "I have hardly been able to think of anything else."

"Nor I. It was more than I could have ever dreamed of. You are so beautiful. I can't wait for tonight."

"We need to be careful. Here comes Patrick."

The existing room which is my bedroom and Emma's is about twelve feet square, and we decided to make the new bedroom twelve feet by fourteen feet to match the kitchen. That would provide space in front of all three rooms for a covered verandah where we could sit or work in fair weather. Patrick sketched out some drawings.

"We still have some old lumber in the barn, but most of it will have to be purchased new. Also, insulation that works better than straw, nails and all the rest. You will want windows also? We should decide how many. Next time I am in Flagstaff, I will consult with my friend at the general store. Perhaps he will give us a deal." Patrick winked. "He is an old friend of mine. You come with me, Luke, when I go, OK? Once we find out how much all of this will cost, we can work out terms together." Luke agreed, and they shook hands on it.

Chapter Fifty-Three

Later that week, I rose early to get ready for my big day with Emma at the sewing bee. It was now September and beginning to feel chilly in the mornings, but the sky remained clear. The tall grass surrounding us was beginning to turn golden. I packed a small bag with a change of clothes for each of us, along with sandwiches for our lunch. I had killed a chicken the day before and made a big pot of stew for my contribution to our evening meal. I was beyond excited for this new adventure and grateful that Luke not only liked the idea of me going but encouraged me.

He hugged me before I got into the wagon and Emma, too, then handed her up to me. I had already stowed the shotgun in the back of the wagon, just in case.

"Have a wonderful time," he said. "I will miss you both."

Emma was full of questions as we made our way to Flagstaff. "Where are we going? Who will be there? What will we do all day? Will there be other children to play with?" and so on. I had no answers for her and simply said, "we will find out. It will be fun, wait and see."

Blue had given me directions to her home, so when we entered Flagstaff we went directly there, instead of to her shop. It was a large, ornate home, quite dark, as she had indicated to me, with a wide verandah encircling two sides of the house. When we entered, there was a large parlor to the left and a smaller room to the right, most likely the dining room, and a stately staircase rising to the upper floors. The wood trim was dark but there was lovely, flowered wallpaper in lighter colors covering the walls in each of the rooms and the entryway.

Blue had explained to me that on the days the bee met, the shop was closed except to members of the bee who might need supplies or new fabric. It was only a few minutes' walk away.

We arrived about 10:00 am., and already several women were getting settled. Blue welcomed Emma and me and began introducing us to the other participants. Two other ladies had brought young children and one of them, Alice, offered to take Emma into the room across the hall where she could play with several children about her age. There were pillows, sets of blocks and dolls to play with. Emma had brought her doll Blue. She seemed content to meet the other children. They were close enough by so any of us could hear if there was a commotion and the children could visit us if they wished.

I brought my chicken stew and lunch for Emma and me into the kitchen. It reminded me of the kitchen in my parent's home, large and well kept. There was an icebox to hold our food, which I appreciated, and a large coal stove on which I could heat my stew in the evening.

Grace had set up three tables in the front room with chairs all around. By the time I settled at one of them, there were seven women besides Grace, Blue and me. Most of us had handwork of some kind, ranging from piecing a small quilt to making a crocheted outfit for an infant. I brought two pillowcases and a small tablecloth to embroider.

There were four women at my table, including me and three at each of the others. I determined to get to know the women at my table to begin with. Alice was to my left. She had two young children, Charlotte and Ethan, ages three and five, who were just then playing with Emma across the hall. Alice was probably in her early thirties and had a pleasant face. She was hand-piecing blocks for a small quilt. Then there was Anne-Marie, an older woman who was working on a crocheted afghan. To my right, Daisy, very obviously expecting, was busy hemming nappies. These three women, I learned, all lived in town, and I found their conversation interesting and I learned a lot about the town of Flagstaff from them. I hoped I would get to know them better in time, as well as the other ladies who were there.

At noon, those of us who had brought lunches took a break to eat. I introduced Emma to the other women, and she ate with us.

About 4:00 pm the group began to break up. Grace and Blue served tea and cookies and by about five everyone had left except me and another young woman, Olivia, from an outlying ranch who planned to stay.

I was pleased to find that several of the ladies made a point of telling me, before they left, they were glad I had come and looked forward to seeing me again. They also complimented Emma on her good behavior. Daisy told me she hoped to know me better and to know more about being a young mother, this being her first child.

I was proud of Emma for behaving so well all day, although by dinnertime, she was getting ready for a melt-down, since she had missed her nap. I spent some time away from the others, holding and talking to her and apparently averted a crisis.

After we had feasted on my chicken stew and the delicious bread that Olivia contributed, I put Emma to bed early in the room Blue showed me. I enjoyed my evening with Blue, Grace, and Olivia and sat up talking with them until well past my usual bedtime, and I finally had the nerve to tell them that I had just become engaged.

"How wonderful", Blue said, which was echoed by the others. "When is the wedding? Tell us about Luke. Give us the details!"

I was embarrassed but told them what I felt comfortable sharing. I did not mention he is mixed blood.

What a treat to have no chores or obligations and to simply enjoy the company of like-minded women! It was nice getting to know Olivia in a quieter setting, too, as she appeared to be quite shy. She told me her family raised sheep on the ranch she came from, processing and selling the wool.

Emma and I returned home the following morning, after enjoying a delicious breakfast of pancakes and fruit, thanks to Grace, and giving a few more details about Luke. I was so grateful to Blue and Grace for introducing me to this group of interesting women. I was determined to become a regular member of this group.

Chapter Fifty-Four

A few weeks later, stones had been laid in the corners to support the sills for the new bedroom and the verandah. They had been fixed in cement. A pile of lumber for the outside walls stood nearby. Windows and roofing could be ordered later. The agreement Patrick had made with us is he would pay for half of everything up front with Luke paying the other half. Then he would then pay Luke and me half wages until we had paid back the remainder of the cost. I thought that was very generous and told Patrick so.

"It only seems fair, lass. Besides, we are all family now."

Of course, everyone knew by now that Luke and I were engaged. You can't keep that kind of information secret in a small community for very long! We were bombarded with well wishes from everyone on the ranch and a few gifts.

It was now mid-September. I was eager to finish the addition before winter came, but of course, the cattle run would be in a few weeks and that took precedence. I kept my fingers crossed and did whatever I could to help. Slowly, the framework of the addition went up along with the outside walls. Boards were laid for the floor inside the new bedroom and for the porch. By late September, the roof was framed and spaces for the windows had been cut. We still needed insulation, inside walls, doors, and windows. But now all hands were needed to prepare for the October cattle run.

I was impatient but had to hold my peace. The room would be finished after the run and hopefully before snow came. There was no other choice. I kept busy with the harvest of the garden, storing the root vegetables and winter squash in the 'cold cellar', drying onions and garlic and herbs, and canning tomatoes, pickled beets, and cucumbers.

And, of course, I continued to spend part of every day, as before, reading to Emma. She was beginning to be able to recognize letters and to pick out words. I made cards for the alphabet and easy words to help teach her to read. She appeared to be bright and was eager to learn. I was so proud of her! I had enjoyed several visits to the library recently with Cora, bringing Emma with us, and had picked out more books suitable to teaching a young child. The set-up of the new sewing machine would have to wait.

The day of the annual cattle run up to the rail line east of Flagstaff, dawned clear and dry. Luke was up early, as were all the other hands and Patrick, himself. The herding dogs were ready and barking their excitement. I had to hold onto Luna to keep her from joining in. Emma and I watched as the run began from the safety of our home.

To my surprise, I heard hoof beats behind our cabin and saw a rider coming over the crest of the hill heading right for me. I wasn't sure at first, but then I saw it was James. He was carrying a rifle. I picked up Emma and grabbed Luna and ran into the house, slamming the front door behind me and shoving the heavy lock into place. I shoved the table against it and then bolted the back door. I stood in the back corner behind the stove. I could barely breath.

"Come out here," James shouted. "Come out here now! I want to talk to you!" He was slurring his words. I said nothing.

"Get out here, bitch! I know what you are doing with my old, so-called friend Luke! I am going to get him for this and then you will be sorry!"

Luna growled and Emma cried but I held my ground.

"Get away from us, James! There is nothing for you here!"

A shot crashed through the front door and I huddled against the floor, with Emma in my arms. Another shot rang out and slammed into the back wall. Luna cried out in pain. Emma began screaming. Then I heard his horse moving away, at a full gallop. I peeked out the door. James was already near the ranch house and heading for the line of men surrounding the cattle. I tried to yell a warning, but of course there was too much noise and my words were lost. I checked on Luna. Her shoulder had been grazed but she was bleeding profusely. I wrapped her shoulder in a towel and held her tight for a few minutes. She calmed somewhat.

I ran outside again holding Emma in my arms. She was still screaming. Patrick was out in front, as usual, but had paused, with his hands up to signal the men to change direction. They slowed down, trying to figure out what was happening. The dogs ran back and forth, guiding and corralling any strays. I had always marveled at their energy and stamina, as well as their intelligence in performing this enormous task but right now I was shaking too hard to notice them. I saw Luke and James's brothers on the near side of the mass of balling animals. It was too far to see the riders on the other side, but I assumed it was the remainder of the men.

Suddenly it looked like James was heading straight for Luke. He was holding his riffle by the barrel and was swinging it like a club. Luke did not see him at first and when James hit him, Luke veered off course and almost lost his balance. I could see him recover and try to evade James. Then I saw Tom and Nat moving forward towards Luke.

From far away I could barely hear James yelling, "I have seen you with my wife, Luke. I have seen you in my house. You have been sleeping there! You are a bastard! You are a dead man!" He was slurring his words, but his meaning was perfectly clear.

Meanwhile, the cattle were surging to the right of both men. Luke recovered his direction and James approached again and hit him, hard, with the butt end of his gun. Luke cut hard to the left, knocking into James's horse and James lost his balance. He fell sideways and was immediately caught by the cattle. He tried to hang on, but a sharp horn caught him in his side and pulled him down. He disappeared under the churning feet.

I watched all of this, not quite understanding what was happening at first, and then, finally, understanding too well. I cried out and my hand went over my mouth in horror.

I collapsed onto my knees, still cradling Emma. I was shaking uncontrollably.

Oh, James, why did you have to return? How could you have been filled with such rage and hate that you had to seek vengeance? Oh, my God—that could have been Luke lying out there!

Patrick apparently did not see what had just happened. However, he knew something was not right. He raised both his hands to signal slowing and then stopping the cattle run. The men and dogs immediately began turning the cattle back towards the coral.

Patrick was soon heading towards Luke. I noticed James's brothers moved forward and alongside Luke, grabbing hold of his horse's bridle. Luke looked badly shaken but was still seated. The throng of cattle finally passed beyond the barn and house but gradually slowed to a walk and formed a circle, guided by the men and dogs. I did not want to see what was under their feet.

As I returned to the cabin to check on Luna, I saw Cora and Julia running up the hill after me. I was moving in a fog, instinctively doing what needed to be done. There were two large bullet holes through the front door and two bullets lodged in the back door. Luna was shaking and whimpering. I grabbed a clean towel and carefully unwrapped the first to examine the wound. Cora and Julia arrived just as I was starting to clean Luna's bloody gash. Julia put a kettle of water on the stove to boil and I cleaned the wound as well as I could through her long hair, while Cora held her gently. When the water was boiling, I wet the towel to do a better job. Using my sewing scissors, I cleared the hair from the area. It looked like the bullet had gone straight through, and had not hit an artery or any bones, which was a blessing. Just a flesh wound and no bullet to have to dig out. Thank the good lord. I do not know what I would do if I lost Luna!

Cora made hot compresses for Luna's shoulder, front and back, and I tied more towels around them to keep them in place. I could see Luna was in pain, but at least she was more relaxed and no longer whimpering. Emma was upset about Luna, of course, but Julia comforted her and eventually she quieted and fell asleep. Cora put her arms around me and said comforting words, but I felt nothing.

That evening, everyone gathered at the ranch house for what would have been our celebration dinner. However, when Patrick announced there had been a terrible accident, resulting in the death of James Parker, no one was in the mood to eat or celebrate. I felt totally numb, just going through the motions of greeting people. Luke stood close to me. He was hunched over and holding his right arm. There was a gash on his forehead and traces of blood on his face. I could see he was in pain.

"I am so sorry, Sarah!" he said. "I didn't see him at first and then, suddenly, there he was, just behind me. He hit me hard several times with some heavy object. It looked like the butt end of his rifle. I think he was trying to kill me! I could hear him yelling something and making threats. Then he disappeared and was under the feet of the cattle. It all happened so fast. I do not know what happened!"

"I do," I said calmly, as if from far away. "I saw what happened. James came back to claim what he thought was his. He came first to our cabin and tried to kill me and Emma, but I locked myself inside with her and Luna and we hid behind the stove. He did hit Luna, a flesh wound. He said some terrible things and then he headed towards you. He was very drunk. It was a one-sided fight between you and him. He lost. It is as it should be. Do not fret." I leaned against Luke. We were both shaking.

Nat and Tom hovered nearby, holding their hats, clearly unsure what to say. Then Patrick came over to where we were standing.

"Luke, are you alright? You look hurt. And Sarah–I heard shots. Are you and Emma OK?"

I will be OK," Luke said. "Just badly bruised, I think. Thanks for asking. James shot at Sarah and Emma and hit Luna."

"Cora and Julia came to help me bandage Luna."

"It seems clear that James was very drunk and out of control.," Patrick said. "You are lucky that he did not kill either of you. I thought this sad business was over, but I can see James still held hatred and the thought off revenge in his heart."

"I thought Emma and I were done for when James came for us. At least now, I am truly free," I managed to say. "No more looking over my shoulder. He is really gone." Then something inside of me cracked and I surprised myself by bursting into tears. What is this? Why am I crying? I should feel relieved. Instead, I just sobbed.

So much for our engagement celebration!

"Let me take you home, my love," said Luke. I was relieved to take his arm and return to the cabin, with Emma. The three of us walked silently up the hill. Neither of us had the heart to tell Emma her father was dead.

Chapter Fifty-Five

Thankfully, there was no inquiry and no inquest regarding James's death. It was simply a terrible accident. The books at the Flagstaff courthouse were closed. The cattle run was postponed for a few weeks. Nat and Tom took James's remains back to New Hampshire for burial. Before they left, they came to say goodbye and to see their niece Emma. She gave each of them a big hug when they picked her up.

"I can't tell you how sorry we are about the way this whole thing came down," Nat said, ruefully, while Tom picked up Emma and hugged her.

Tom agreed, saying, "There is no way to understand or explain what happened to James. Something must have snapped in him."

"It does not matter now but thank you for saying that. Will you be coming back to the ranch sometime?

"We have not decided yet," said Nat. "Patrick has asked us to return. In case we do not, we wish you all the best whatever happens now."

I kissed each of them on the cheek and we said our goodbyes. This ugly business had finally come to a end.

I wrote to my parents and family to tell them what had happened. I received a lovely letter in return, saying in part, *"Now you are finally free to follow your heart wherever it may lead. If it is Luke, you have our full-hearted blessing. If it is somewhere else, the same is true. Just let us know where your choices lead you. Always know how much we love you!"*

I showed this letter to Luke. "My heart leads me to you!" I told him.

Chapter Fifty-Six

Eventually, work continued on the construction of the extra room and a covered verandah along the front of the cabin. We also decided to break through the back wall of the middle room and make a tighter back wall with deep, floor to ceiling shelves against it. That would provide much needed storage space for my fabric, sewing supplies, and other household needs. Now we had a cabin thirty-six feet long by fourteen feet, with doors inside between the rooms and access to the verandah from each room. Several new windows let in lots of light, and the entire space felt airy. What a luxury to have so much space! I found that thought amusing, considering the home I had been raised in.

When we moved the bed into the new room, I made it up with my mother's beautiful quilt on top. The many colors seemed to dance across the quilt, and it brightened up the room. I loved it. Emma already had her grandmother's special quilt on her bed to keep her snug and warm this winter. It was made in shades of blue and white. Both quilts brought back happy memories of our visit the previous winter.

The next time I attended the monthly sewing bee in Flagstaff, Grace and Blue helped me load my beautiful 'new' sewing machine into the wagon. We had to tie it securely with ropes so it would not be damaged on the bumpy road back to the ranch. Emma was as excited as I was by our new treasure. It was now late November, and I was grateful we could get everything arranged before the snows came.

Blue gifted me with several yards of fabric suitable for infants and toddlers, including lovely soft flannels, along with the supplies I would need to get started. I purchased additional fabric, as well since winter was coming. I could not wait to begin designing and sewing little outfits. I already had some ideas of what I wanted to make. I decided to start with a warm nightgown for Emma and something soft and pretty for baby Rosy. Those would be simple enough for me to practice on. Eventually I would make things for Blue's and Grace's shop. I could even make soft crib quilts out of my scraps. We had yet to discuss how that would work financially, but I had no doubt we could come to a fair arrangement.

All through that winter, with no gardening to keep me busy, I spent many days sewing. I continued to read to Emma and took advantage of her naps to read to myself. When Christmas came, I presented Cora with a flannel sleeping sack for the baby, who was now about four months old. It had a hood and was closed at the bottom with pink ribbons for easy changing.

"Oh, Sarah." She said, with pleasure. "How perfect for these cold winter nights! It is lovely." I showed her what I had made for Emma–a long flannel nightgown in pale blue with matching booties and a cap. Cora marveled. "It seems you have more skills than you have been letting on. Little outfits and warm winter wear will be perfect for Blue's shop. Congratulations!"

Cora's words gave me a warm feeling that was new to me. I knew I was good with the farm work, but this was an accomplishment that was much more personal. My heart sang.

In January, we had a small celebration for Emma's fourth birthday at the ranch house. There was a high wind, and it was bitter cold, but we all dressed snugly. It was nice to share this celebration with Patrick, Cora, and their children, and, of course, Luke. Little Rosy stole the show even though it was Emma's birthday.

Luke continued to join me and Emma for dinner and to visit for a while before heading back to the barn for the night. I loved our long talks, and our fevered goodnight kisses. And the more I thought about Luke and what our lives could be together, the more convinced I became that I wanted to be with him for the rest of my life.

"I have been thinking," I said to Luke one evening.

"What have you been thinking?"

"I have been thinking we should start planning a wedding!"

"I think that is a wonderful idea!" said Luke, grinning and taking me in his arms and swinging me right off my feet. "I thought you would never ask!! Let's plan a wedding and invite all your friends and everyone on the ranch and have a grand celebration!"

"And my family, too! I want Mama and Ben and everyone else in my family to come if they can. Lord knows where they will stay, but we will figure that out. Oh Luke, it will be such a happy time! How about a small wedding now and then a big celebration in the spring? A beautiful, spring wedding. Let's make the announcement tonight!"

I stood with Luke beside our cabin, my arm around his waist. Emma was holding his other hand and Luna, still limping but healing well, lay in the sun on our new verandah. Looking down over the barn and ranch house below, with the sun high over the tall pines and the beautiful mountains beyond, I was content.

In my mind's eye, I saw a young boy riding a pony bareback, with his father on his own horse beside him. The boy had long black hair and sat straight and proud. He was laughing and his father laughed with him. Then I saw Emma, a few years older, playing with a puppy which looked just like Luna when she was little. They chased each other through the long grass, giggling and yipping. An infant was lying near me in a basket wrapped in a soft multicolored quilt. Her dark eyes were wide open, taking everything in.

Timeline, Book II, Hannah's Legacy

1845-1904

This Timeline follows the important dates and events in Hannah Stones life and continues with her descendants up to 1904. Important or interesting historic events that would have had a bearing on her life and the times in which she and her family lived are also included.

1845-1860

1846	*Elias Howe was granted a patent on his new sewing machine in Hartford, CT. It was the first sewing machine in the United States and was used in factory assembly lines.*
1850	Caroline Rachel Horner marries Jacob Matthew Applegate (1830-1861)
	They have one living child after several miscarriages and a still birth: Hannah Rebecca Applegate (1858-1951)
1850s	*Sewing machine production became widespread, with the first salable machines being made by Isaac Singer and used commercially.*
1856	*A quotation in Godey's Ladies' Book states: "Next to the plough, this sewing machine is perhaps humanity's most blessed instrument."*

1860-1900

1860s	*Sewing machines were first purchased by the public, especially by women. Work that took 14 ½ hours (such as making a man's shirt) was reduced to one hour by machine. Isaak Singer was the first entrepreneur of sewing machines that could be purchased on a monthly payment plan.*
1861	*The Civil War Begins*
1861	**Matthew Applegate enlists in the Union Army and is killed 6 months later in Tennessee. His body is never found.**
1862	**Caroline Applegate catches fever and dies.**
1862	**Hannah is taken to live with "Aunt Rebecca" Horner, and Rebecca raises her.**
1877	**Hannah Applegate marries Aaron Matthew Benson (1857-1883)**
	They have two children:
	Jacob William Benson (1878-1960)
	Sarah Rachel Benson (1881-1954)
1883	**Aaron Benson is killed in a freak lumbering accident.**
1887	**Hannah Applegate Benson marries Benjamin Whitmore Stone (1855-1939)**
	They have four children:

Rebecca Caroline Stone (1888- 1969)

Lydia Jane Stone (1890-1968)

Benjamin Thomas Stone (1892 -1918)

Margaret Abigail Stone (1895 -1985)

1888	*Kodak introduces the first easy to use box camera, with the slogan "You push the button, we do the rest!"*
1889	*First electrified sewing machine invented.*
1895	**Ben Stone finishes building a new seven-bedroom house and barns for his family on the main street of the village.**
1898	**Sarah Benson goes west to the Arizona Territories with her fiancé, James Parker. They marry in June when they arrive in Flagstaff. They are hired to work on the Copper Stallion Ranch.**

They have one child:

Emma Louise Parker (January, 1899-   )

1900

1900	*Kodak introduces the first Brownie camera. It is an inexpensive "point and shoot."*
Early 1900s	*Electric sewing machines became popular and generally available to the public.*

Fall 1900	Sarah is almost killed by James Parker near the ranch in AZ. Her unborn son does not survive.
1901-02	Sarah and Emma visit family in NH. for six months. Sarah obtains a divorce from James. They return to the ranch in June.
1903	Sarah and Luke become engaged.

End Book II of Hannah's Legacy

About the Author:

Cary Flanagan has been a quilter since 1991. After a twenty-year career in Mental Health and Social Services she left full-time work in 2004 to become a quilt pattern designer, author, and teacher. She established Something Sew Fine Quilt Design at that time. Her quilt patterns sell nationally and Internationally.

Cary was born and raised in Cambridge Massachusetts, but moved to New Hampshire in 1972, where she and husband purchased and renovated an 1840's farm house and barn. She has spent almost every summer of her life at the "little log cabin by the lake" and the small village in New Hampshire where her family spent their summers and where part of this story is set. She has also spent time exploring parts of northern Arizona, including the area around Flagstaff where most of this story is set. These are places she knows well and loves.

Cary holds a BA in Sociology and Anthropology and an M.Ed. in Counseling. She lives in southern New Hampshire with her husband Ron and their much-loved rescue dog, Nyxie.

For more information, go to www.caryflanagan.com or to www.somethingsewfine.com. You can also visit Cary on Facebook and Instagram.

Watch for
Book III of Hannah's Legacy,
coming Spring 2023

After the Storm
the Story of Hannah Applegate
Benson Stone.

Book I of Hannah's Legacy

If you have not yet read the first novel in this trilogy, "After the Storm", here is an excerpt from the first chapter of this heartfelt fictional memoir:

"Life can be very cruel sometimes. I have suffered many losses in my time, but I have so many memories of good times past and they help to make up for the hard times.

I have been truly blessed in my ninety-two years. I was raised by a remarkable and gifted aunt; I have loved and been loved by two good men and have born six children who have graced and filled my world in ways it is difficult to express. And I have been luckier than most women of my time to have been able to spend my days and years doing those things I have always loved best, raising my children, sewing and creating beautiful quilts, cultivating my gardens, giving love and assistance where I could, and living my faith. I have truly lived a good life and I am grateful.

I was born August 14, 1858, just a few years before the terrible war between the north and south, though, of course I did not know anything about that until much later. I was born in an old farmhouse near a small village not far from the White Mountains of New Hampshire. My parents' farm was small – just a few acres. It wasn't much compared to some. There were not many families in the village itself at that time, (our little town did not begin to grow and prosper until after the railroad was built right through the center of it some years later), but it was the kind of place where everyone looked out for everyone else, including those, like my parents, who lived in the surrounding hills and valleys.

My earliest real memory is of my mother crying inconsolably. I was perhaps three or four. Other people had come to the house, but no one would tell me why she was crying until finally my Aunt Rebecca gently set me on her lap and told me that my mother was very sad. I vaguely remembered when my father went away with a lot of other men from the village, and my mother held me up and waved my arm to the men marching by. My mother was very sad then too, but this was different, somehow. My Aunt tried to explain that my father had gone far away to fight in a war and would never be able to come home. I wanted to know why, but she just cried then, too.

Not long after that my mother became very ill. The shades were always drawn in her bedroom and Aunt Rebecca stayed in the house to take care of her. I would slip into Mama's room and lie beside her, but she was asleep most of the time. I do not even think she knew I was there. And then she went 'far away' the way my papa did. Lots of people came to visit our house. They brought food with them and said "poor child" to me. I did not know why.

Aunt Rebecca took me to live with her in the house in the village she had inherited from her parents. At first, I did not want to go in case my mother came back and could not find me, but my Aunt said everything would be all right, so I went with her. It was a fine house, painted white, much bigger, and nicer than my own house and I liked being there. There was an upstairs and a downstairs and a wide covered veranda on the front of the house where you could sit and watch folks going by. And I had my very own bedroom. "This was your mother's bedroom when she was growing up", Aunt Rebeca told me. "And now it is yours." That was a comfort to me, but I was still confused about what would happen when my mother came back to get me."

My Aunt seemed to me to be very wise and even tempered, but not very happy. She had a warm manner that put me at ease some of the time, but she also seemed pinched and standoffish, at times, which I did not understand. It was as if she shifted from one personality to another. She was quite tall (of course everyone is very tall when you are a little girl) and stood very straight. She always wore dark dresses with a very high neck and long sleeves, even in summer, and her dark hair was pulled back severely in a knot at the back. She smelled like lavender. Her face did not have much color and she did not smile often but when she did smile her features softened. I wished she would smile more often.

In the first few weeks that I was in that house I asked my Aunt several times when I would see my mother again. "Will she take me back to the farm to live when she comes to get me, or will we live here?" Eventually, when my Aunt could not give me a good answer, I stopped asking. I missed my Mama very much. And at night I was scared, all alone in the dark. I didn't feel safe. Sometimes I cried myself to sleep.

I remember two recurring nightmares that

haunted me during most of my childhood. In one I was falling endlessly through dark clouds with nothing to catch hold of to anchor me. All around me was rain, flashes of lightning and the booming sounds of thunder. In the other dream, I was in an endless tunnel that was just big enough for my small body to crawl through. There was dim light, so I could see there was no end to it, no way out. Often, I woke up screaming and in a cold sweat after one of these dreams. My Aunt would come quickly to reassure me. "Nothing can harm you here", she would tell me, and she would stay with me until I went back to sleep.

Aunt Rebecca helped me get settled in the house and took me walking around the village. She introduced me to the chickens running around behind the house and the two goats which gave us milk. I also met her large grey mare, a sweet-tempered horse named "Jewel". She pulled Aunt Rebecca's wagon. I was allowed to sit on her back sometimes as a special treat. My aunt told me that Jewel had a baby every few years and that if I wanted, when I was old enough, I could keep one of the babies to take care of myself! I could hardly wait to meet my own baby horse....

..."Sometimes when my aunt took me with her shopping, I could see the expressions on people's faces when they looked at me. Most seemed kind and welcomed me to the village, but sometimes I could hear them whisper words behind us like "poor little orphan" as we walked down the street.

"What is an orphan?" I asked my aunt.

"An orphan," she explained gently, "is somebody who does not have a mama or a papa. Someone like you. Don't pay them any mind, they mean no harm. Besides," she continued, "you have me now, and soon you will have lots of friends of your own to keep you company....

..."I began to notice a change in Aunt Rebecca from when I first came. She seemed more relaxed. The lines in her face softened and she moved with a lighter step. I even noticed she smiled more than when I first arrived. My aunt was so thoughtful and loving that I began, eventually, to think of her as my mother, and she told me often how glad she was that I had come. The first time she said that I pressed my face against her warm body and hugged her. I had no words for how I felt."

For more information and to order a copy of After the Storm, please click on

www.caryflanagan.com